1000 BEST

job hunting secrets

DIANE STAFFORD
& MORITZA DAY

SOURCEBOOKS, INC.
NAPERVILLE, ILLINOIS

P9-DOE-641

LAKE COUNTY PUBLIC LIBRARY

3 3113 02330 4951

Copyright © 2004 by Diane Stafford and Moritza Day
Cover and internal design © 2004 by Sourcebooks, Inc.
Sourcebooks and the colophon are registered trademarks of
Sourcebooks, Inc.

All rights reserved. No part of this book may be reproduced in
any form or by any electronic or mechanical means including
information storage and retrieval systems—except in the case of
brief quotations embodied in critical articles or reviews—without permission in writing from its publisher, Sourcebooks, Inc.

This publication is designed to provide accurate and authorita-
tive information in regard to the subject matter covered. It is sold
with the understanding that the publisher is not engaged in rendering legal, accounting, or other professional service. If legal
advice or other expert assistance is required, the services of a
competent professional person should be sought.—*From a Dec-
laration of Principles Jointly Adopted by a Committee of the American Bar Association and a Committee of Publishers and
Associations*

Published by Sourcebooks, Inc.
P.O. Box 4410, Naperville, Illinois 60567-4410
(630) 961-3900
FAX: (630) 961-2168
www.sourcebooks.com

Library of Congress Cataloging-in-Publication Data

Stafford, Diane.
  1000 best job hunting secrets / By Diane Stafford and Moritza
Day.
      p. cm.
  Includes bibliographical references.
  ISBN 1-4022-0218-0 (alk. paper)
  1. Resumes (Employment) I. Title: Best Job Hunting Secrets. II.
Title: One thousand best job hunting secrets. III. Day, Moritza. IV.
Title.
HF5383.S714 2004
650.14'2—dc22
                          2004001032

Printed and bound in the United States of America
         VP   10 9 8 7 6 5 4 3 2 1

LAKE COUNTY PUBLIC LIBRARY

To job seekers everywhere, "resume up,"
and find your dream job!

ACKNOWLEDGMENTS

Our sincere appreciation to these people for making this book a reality:

Hillel Black, Sourcebooks editor, who inspired this book and gave us support and direction.

New England Publishing Associates' Ed Knappman, for his professionalism and excellence.

Sarah Tucker, Morgan Hrejsa, and Megan Dempster of Sourcebooks, who ably shepherded *1000 Best Job Hunting Secrets* through the editing and production process.

Barbi Pecenco, publicist extraordinaire of Sourcebooks, whose spirit and enthusiasm are huge assets.

Diane Stafford also thanks:

Jennifer Shoquist San Luis, my extraordinary daughter.

Robert San Luis, my terrific son-in-law.

Chris Fleming, my dear friend who supports me every step of the way.

Jay Diamonon, for sending me Moritza.

Plus my friends and family, whom I love dearly: Benjamin San Luis, David Ludington, Dan Rader, David Nordin, Allen Shirley, Camilla Pierce, Eddi Lee, Christina Shirley, Gina and Curtis Bradley, Clinton Shirley, Richard Pierce, Russell Kridel, M.D., Michael Allison, Scott Coleman, Dot and Laurens Horstman, Elizabeth Frost Knappman, Renee Somoza, Dinah Anderson, Tessie Patterson, Rachel Capote, Trey Speegle, Dana and Clarence Chandler,

Spiker Davis, Doug and Karen Johnson, Brett and Shari Belmarez, JoAnn Roberson, Donna Pate, Tom Swan, Jean Hardy, Bob Livermore, Angela Clark, Jami Appenzeller, Gabi Ventura, Dennis Doughty, Evin Thayer, Lisa Hamilton, Blair Pittman, Cameron Liem, Lindsay Liem, Curtis Bradley, Xanthe Shirley, Austin Shirley, Mark Nichols, Tom Sankey, Martin Thornhill.

Moritza Day also thanks:

Meredith West, my sister

Martin, Rosalie, and Malcolm Day, see ya some day.

Jay Diamonon, for recommending this collaboration.

John Goodson, recruiter.

Steve Tatar, recruiter.

Linda Maitland, Ph.D., for continued encouragement.

Gwen Cherry for assistance, friendship, and fun.

Rebecca Rucker, for wisdom and wit.

Linda Stiles, fellow speaker and writer and one of the most patient women in the world.

Buddy Bailey, advisor and friend.

Sally Rand Day, beloved gato, friend, family, and loved one.

DISCLAIMER

This book contains the authors' opinions and ideas. It is intended to provide helpful and informative material on the subject matter covered herein, and is sold with the understanding that the authors and the publisher are not engaged in rendering professional services or counseling via the book. If the reader wants personal guidance or advice, he or she should seek an in-person consultation with a competent professional. This is a supplement, not a replacement, for advice from a career counselor, professional, or recruiter. The authors and publisher specifically disclaim any responsibility for any liability, loss, or risk, whether personal, financial, or otherwise, that someone may incur as a consequence, directly or indirectly, of the use and application of any of the contents of this book. Also, responsibility for any adverse effects that result from the use of information in this book rests solely with the reader.

TABLE OF CONTENTS

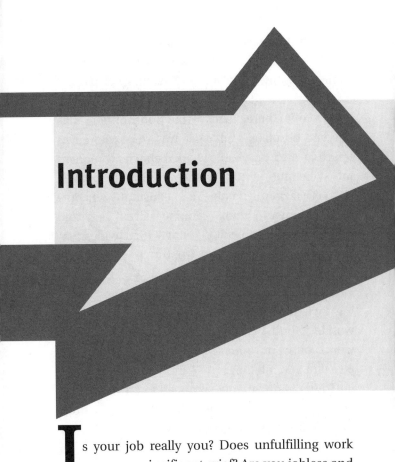

Introduction

Is your job really you? Does unfulfilling work cause you significant grief? Are you jobless and terrified of the mysterious "job hunt" you're undertaking?

It's hard to be happy about work that's nothing but bring-home-the-bacon. You want satisfaction, excitement, great bosses, fun coworkers, and big money isn't bad, either. And if you get laid off, you want something new, pronto. Like many workers in America today, you may even keep your resume up-to-date, just in case something interesting comes along.

When it comes to jobs, this is a self-indulgent era. We want it all. Few of us work forty years for the same company, and hordes of us make a habit of browsing want ads and Internet job sites, just to see what's out there. The term "job-hopper" has become obsolete, and what was once viewed as irascible and unreliable work behavior (frequent job switching) is now, in the era of *Oprah*, called self-actualization. People are constantly encouraged to unearth their "genuine selves" and find endeavors they can enjoy. Living with a work situation that depresses or frustrates you makes absolutely no sense.

Today, in record numbers, Americans are pursuing their destinies in a fast-paced, ever-changing working world. Because much of your life is spent at work, you want to make sure that those hours are pleasant and fulfilling.

To find a dream job, you need to create a quintessential resume that will rise to the top of a huge stack. You snag an interview by finding a way to set your resume apart from others and the best way to do that is to make it extraordinary.

Showcase your skills and experience and your "rightness" for the job. Make sure that the word *terrific* comes to mind when a hiring manager looks at your resume (either that or *wonderful, outstanding,* or *perfect*) because you've done what it takes to perfect a summation of your work and skills.

Remember, if you're out of work, your job is getting a job. If you're disgruntled with your current work, your job should be finding something better.

And, this will happen if you follow these basic rules for succeeding in the job-search world:

- Determine what you're really good at doing—your core strengths. If you're hazy on these, ask friends or relatives to help you pinpoint the answer. Half of finding a satisfying job is discovering where your strengths lie, and then zeroing in on work that allows you to use and develop those skills. Doing something that comes naturally can motivate you like nothing else; you're almost sure to excel if your job is one that makes the most of your strengths.

- Write a great resume, or if writing is your weak point, get help in writing a great resume (see chapter 23). Ask friends or family to read your resume to make sure it's clear, concise, hard-hitting, and mistake-free.

- Check the Internet for companies that fit your skills. Contact the personnel representatives at those firms and ask if jobs will be opening up anytime soon.

- Go low-tech. Chat up your job-hunt. If friends or relatives can clear your way to a position someone knows of because he works at a certain company, you get to walk into the interview with an asterisk by your name. The hiring manager thinks, "Hey, someone has vouched for this person as a standout employee, so I'll take a long look at him."

- Call up an old employer and ask if he needs you to work as a consultant.

- Devote full eight-hour workdays to your job hunt. Just because you've been laid off, or you haven't worked in years doesn't mean a leisurely approach will find you a great job. Be assertive and aggressive. Go for it just like you would if your money were running out this week.
- Explore fields that need employees desperately; in 2003–2004, you actually get a signing bonus for going into nursing. There's also a huge push on getting people into teaching. And the federal government is an especially ripe field because half of federal workers will reach retirement age in the next five years (2004–09), according to Michelle Conlin, Working Life editor of *Business Week Magazine*. In an interview with Charlie Gibson on *Good Morning America*, she cited the following median salaries: nursing, $44,840; teaching, $43,262; and federal government jobs, $54,656.
- Prep yourself for the moment when your resume strikes a responsive chord and you get a call. If you're the nervous, jittery type, write down what you're going to say and keep it by the phone, along with a copy of your resume. What if you get a call for a mini-screening phone interview and you can't remember a thing you put on your resume? You want to sound smooth, calm, and professional, and if you're not naturally that way, plan your responses so that the first phone encounter with a hiring individual will be close to perfect. If you don't prepare, the stammering alone may

extinguish any interest from the company representative. He may think, "Well, this person can write a good resume, but he sounds clueless on the phone—I'll pass on asking him to come in for an interview." What you want is the opposite scenario—the brief phone chat heightens the hiring manager's interest so that his thought process is, "Wow, he seemed promising just from the resume, and he sounds even better on the phone. I'm very interested in talking to this man."

- Stay on task. Your job search should be a top priority, right up there with family responsibilities. Use a day planner to keep track of people you've contacted, what you've said in the cover letters and resumes (what if you forget what you said you could do for them?), and when you said you would call to make sure the resumes were received. Obviously, you must make sure that you're absolutely flawless about keeping interview appointments straight; leave home early so that you're either a bit early or on time (far better to be fifteen minutes early than fifteen minutes late). Some hiring managers simply won't hire a person who shows up late for an interview, even if it turns out that candidate spins miracles at the interview table. They believe that tardiness sends an accurate message about that candidate's likelihood of being a good employee.

- Prepare for each interview as if it were your best job possibility. Do your homework on the company. Dress wonderfully. Be immaculately groomed. And follow the interview pointers listed in chapter 28. Before you leave, thank the interviewer for his time, and as soon as you get home, write a thank-you note (see chapter 15 for tips on ways to show appreciation).

- Work on your confidence. Nothing is worse for a resume, cover letter, or interview, than being tentative: "I think I can do this job, but I'm not really sure." Instead, beef up your confidence with daily self-talk: "I am a great candidate for this job, and I want my resume to help me get my foot in the door so I can convince the hiring manager. I'm a real catch as an employee." If negative thoughts creep into your mind, banish them immediately. Don't let old fears and failures trip you up.

BEFRIEND THE INTERNET

Do make the most of low-tech modes (word of mouth and networking), but also be prepared when an employer asks you to send an e-resume or fill out an application online. Most large companies use high-tech devices such as resume scanning software and applicant tracking systems to evaluate prospective employees, which means that job scavengers need to stay abreast of trends and dinosaurs. Sending in a resume that looks like it should have perished in the Ice Age won't help your image in today's Internet-invested workplace.

Look at it this way. The Internet provides some major job-searching advantages. Day and night, you can search databases for suitable job openings, and your information is available 24/7 to company computers that are scanning for the right employees. The downside is that you may have to fill out company website forms that require you to list salary expectations, which locks you into that box when you go in for an interview. Furthermore, the computer won't give you points for charm. If you don't scan well (not enough keywords or jobs or degrees), you may get shut out.

KNOW THE BASICS

You'll hear lots of opinions on what a resume should be, but stick with these universal truths and you (and your resume) will succeed. When it comes to resume writing, distribution, reaction, and follow-up, you need to know:

- Why your resume hasn't worked for you so far
- What you can do to improve it
- How you can customize your resume for various jobs and situations
- How you can make sure your resume does not end up in the trash can
- How you can ensure that your resume gets you an interview
- What you should do after the resume is in the right hands
- Why it's smart to keep tweaking your resume even though you have a job you like
- How to prepare an e-resume
- Why having a scannable resume is important

To do a terrific job, you must understand scannable keywords and e-resumes so that you won't miss out on the good opportunities that come with working the Internet. This knowledge comes in handy whether you're a professional resume writer, a brand-new grad, a laid-off job searcher, or a worker wannabe who has been long gone from the workplace (raising children, globe-trotting, doing senior retirement things). Just keep following up on print ads and tack on the multitude of e-opportunities.

WHERE DO YOU STAND?

On employer rating lists, do you know where you fit in? Are you highly sought after, a candidate that many employers would die to recruit? Or are you in the ranks of those who are looking at fewer opportunities and have skinnier skills lists? In truth, you don't have to be an A-list job hunter to find a great job. If you can write a good resume, you place yourself in the running for lots of positions that you may have previously believed were out of your league.

A hiring manager wants to know about your long-term potential. Will your career grow? Are you a candidate who can work his way up in the company? Will you need a great deal of tutoring in the business to get you up to speed? With these questions buzzing in the minds of hiring managers, your resume must plant a seed of promise—the idea that you are as strong an employee as the resume is substantial.

The message in your resume should be that you want to learn everything you can about the business. You're willing to take on extra responsibility, and you're not someone who refuses to do things that aren't in the official job description. You believe that getting a project out the door is the entire staff's business, and you don't mind pitching in to help coworkers. A helpful, upbeat attitude is a huge plus in the workplace, and if you can make sure that ace comes across when someone reads your resume, you'll get an interview.

On the flip side of that coin, hiring managers look at weak resumes as indicative of low growth potential, little initiative, and lack of a strong work ethic. If you're a real catch as an employee, they assume that you will put some real effort into producing a great resume. Unfortunately, some people who do have excellent skills are overconfident on the subject: "Hey, I'm so outstanding I'm sure I'll get the job, and that's when I'll bother to show how terrific I am. No one cares about resumes." This is like assuming that you don't need to dress well for a first date because you can always turn on your fashion sense later, after you get the person hooked. In either case—a date or a job—it's naïve to underestimate the importance of first impressions. They count.

In your resume, you want to give an employer a very low-risk feeling about hiring you. Training an employee costs lots of money, so when a hiring manager sticks his neck out, he wants to know that it's a safe bet. That's one reason your resume gets scrutinized very carefully when you go in for an interview.

CREATE A DEAL-MAKER

In the great stacks of resumes for a given job, yours should jump out of the batch. The first look at a resume lasts only a few seconds, and following that, the hiring manager discards most and saves only a few to examine more closely. If you make it to the small stack, your resume probably will get passed around to several people involved in hiring, or your potential coworkers. Your resume must be able to survive group inspection, which requires general excellence that pleases all the people all the time, as well as specificity that addresses the job opening and flaunts skills that match the job. You'll know you've succeeded when you revise your resume to the point that you start getting calls to interview for jobs you want.

When reviewing your resume, picture a hiring manager sorting through hundreds of resumes for a job opening. This is only one part of that individual's busy day, and it may be his or her least favorite duty. You want to grab his or her attention with an outstanding resume—not irritate him or her with a bad one that leaves out important information, or is thirty pages long and laughable.

Have empathy for the person on the other end of your resume. Present words that distinguish you as a worthy candidate who will make the company a better place: more profitable, more comfortable, more efficient, and/or more productive.

PAVE THE WAY TO AN INTERVIEW

Fine-tuning a resume is a smart investment. When you go in for an interview, having worked on a resume makes you more familiar with your qualifications. When the hiring manager says, "What do you consider your greatest strengths?" you're all ready to trot out your answer because you've recently spent time pondering that very question.

Naturally, being tongue-tied or unsure in an interview can be a deal-breaker. You don't get much time to bowl over the hiring manager, and if you fumble, he may see you as lacking in confidence. Few interviewers try to pry information out of you, but they do make note when you say something thoughtless or forget a key aspect of job-hunting, such as asking for the job. (See chapter 28 for interview tips.)

So, who gets the job? It may not be the most qualified candidate, but it will almost always be the candidate who puts together an impressive resume, interviews well, and leaves the hiring manager with a positive feeling about having him join the company. Show initiative, follow-through, confidence, and get in there and close the sale. Having done the work beforehand—preparing a strong resume— you're in a great position to raise the interviewer's interest. A hiring manager often bases his questions on things you list in your resume's skills summary (see more on skills summaries, page 23), which gives you a chance to brag about ways that you have benefited companies in the past.

TEAM UP WITH RECRUITERS

Professionals who specialize in job-search activities can expedite your quest. A recruiter, whether a headhunter or in-house company recruiter, is a screener for a company, and he saves everyone time by ferreting out good job candidates who have submitted resumes and merit moving forward to the next stage. Recruiters are quick to cite the obvious pitfalls of poor resumes and careless job searches:

1. Your resume may have vague job descriptions, which make it almost impossible to tell what you've done in the past.
2. You may be applying for every job you see listed, many of which are not at all appropriate or even remotely in the realm of reality. You don't want to be one of the many job searchers who mistakenly think they are qualified for positions for which they would never be legitimate contenders.
3. Your resume may be generic. Remember that you are in a jungle of resumes—hiring personnel receive tons of them. The competition is stiff, so your resume must stand out clearly.

A recruiter can also be your liaison when you're planning a career change. He can explain to a prospective employer your desire to cross over to another field. Perhaps you're working in one field while acquiring the education for another. The recruiter representing you can tell employers that you want to work part time, full time, or intern to gain experience while completing your studies. A situation that may sound iffy or untenable (or like begging) when you present it can sound perfectly logical when a recruiter tactfully pitches it to an employer.

If you don't want a recruiter to act as intermediary, you can certainly try the old-fashioned way and do your own pitch. Look for companies in your area of expertise by visiting the placement office of a school (university, community college, vocational or trade school), or browse the Internet. Once you zero in on a company or two that you want to approach, call and make a proposal. Let the hiring manager know that he would be gaining a high-energy, enthusiastic employee who is willing to work on an interim basis, and if the company likes your work, you would like to stay on and grow with the organization. You're a great bargain!

WRITE A RESUME THAT RAISES EYEBROWS (IN A GOOD WAY)

Always remember the importance of walking in the door with a strong presentation. Recruiters and hiring managers find it strange that people who are searching for jobs are willing to be tenacious about practically anything except writing and refining an excellent resume. The tendency is to get out the old one—whether written in 1980 or 1995 or scribbled on the back of a cocktail napkin—spruce it up, tack on recent jobs, and throw it in an envelope with a cover letter. And then you sit back and wonder why your phone remains silent and nothing cool hits your email inbox.

Headhunters say that far too many job seekers are terrible at writing resumes. Are you one of these people missing the mark? You may inadvertently hide or camouflage your best work attributes, or, at the very least, fail to highlight them. So, the prospective employer gets bad vibes from the start because you aren't making a promising first impression. He figures, *If this person doesn't know enough to understand the importance of presenting himself well in a resume, how can creativity, dependability, and intelligence be parts of the package?*

Fortunately, though, it's easy to give your resume a fixer-upper—either that, or bring out the wrecking ball, demolish it completely, and start from scratch. Whether you are hunting for your very first job, seeking a better position, or planning to rejoin the workforce after raising kids or taking a mini-retirement, this book can help you pull off the best resume possible.

This book is for employed people who are looking for better jobs, the jobless who keep striking out, working-world greenhorns, and people who are happily employed but want to keep their resumes up to snuff just in case the "perfect" job comes along. It contains nuts-and-bolts information that can move you from the Sadly Unemployed Outer Circle to the Happily Employed Inner Circle.

Of course, certain accepted basics always apply, but there are new and different ways to help you target (and snag) a certain job. You may be worried about having to create several versions of the same resume, but this is easy if you have access to a computer. If you're new to the computer, and you need to hustle some resumes out the door, this probably isn't the time to learn computer skills. Instead, just use a typewriter, or find a professional writer or resume writer and hire that person to do the job on a computer. Do ask professional resume writers for references and check with former clients about their experiences. Also, ask what the resume writer's services include. Will he create one resume and that's it? Or is the resume writer willing to turn out resumes customized to suit various job listings? Do you get a copy of the resume on disk? How many hard copies? (See professional resume preparers in chapter 23.)

THINK OUT OF THE BOX

Don't forget that the realm of jobs open to you goes far beyond just the ones you see advertised in pub-lications and on the Internet. What about those jobs that will soon be advertised? You can contact people in the industry you want to enter and ask when job openings are expected. A hiring manager may divulge the scoop on job availability at his company by telling you he expects an opening next month. For all he knows, you're a superb candidate with just the right skills. The extra lead-time allows you to tweak your resume to fit the position and have a resume in the mail before other job hunters even know the opening exists.

When you think resumes, remember three key facets—creating a resume that's best for you; designing the resume to get the attention of a per-son who will be interviewing; and making the resume fit a specific job. Keep in mind that a skill set can bend and change in lots of different ways. Maybe you fine-tuned your people skills while working as a low-on-the-totem-pole phone person who contacted deadbeats for a tiny loan company, and you wonder what that's worth. Well, that ability can carry over into more rarefied workplaces—you can indeed apply for a job as an office manager and use those hard-earned people skills to get you in the door for an interview. The point is, don't assume that every single person who applies for the office manager job has experience in doing exactly that simply because the job listing *asks* for experience as an office manager. Often, what a company asks for and what it gets are two different things. If you get an interview and go in there and wow them with your people skills, organizational ability, and leadership affinity, you may well walk away with the job.

If you're seeking a new position or even plan to switch careers altogether, this book contains essential how-to's on resume writing: the what-it-must-contain and the ways to make yours stand out among legions of others.

Essentially, the five biggest mistakes that you can make when looking for a job are:

- Having a flimsy, incomplete, or generic resume
- Failing to include a great cover letter with a resume
- Failing to network (always remember to tell family, friends, and acquaintances you want job leads)
- Bombing the interview (interviewing the interviewer instead of selling yourself, and forgetting

to express interest in the job)

- Asking an interviewer about salary, vacation, overtime, or benefits before he makes you a job offer (*tres gauche!*)

This book can steer you past land mines and straight to the job that will make you happy. No matter what kinds of problems you've had in the past in your jobs and job searches, this is a new day. Writing a great resume that makes you shine on paper is oh-so-doable. Trust us. We can set you up for success.

1.

Create an Irresistible Resume

People argue about what constitutes a "proper" resume, and, frankly, opinions are all over the map. But the one thing that unquestionably sets an Irresistible Resume apart is that it singles out the job candidate from a crowd of candidates and takes him one step closer to the position he wants. Write a superb resume, and chances are very good that you will get an interview. At the very least, the hiring manager will be curious about the individual who composed such a standout resume.

More than anything else, your resume makes a first impression. If your resume is professional and reflects competence and confidence, the hiring manager sees you as a job seeker who merits closer attention. Conversely, if you whip out a hasty, slipshod resume that doesn't begin to reflect your personal excellence, you literally sell yourself short.

When career strategists coach job seekers, one key element they emphasize is turning out the right resume. Think of your resume as a powerful calling card. Imagine that you are the one perusing stacks of resumes for a given job, and consider how greatly you might be influenced by the positive impact of a well-worded, hard-hitting, smart resume. Instantly, that resume gets placed in the short stack of must-sees.

The four things an Irresistible Resume must do are:
- Seize the interviewer's attention
- Sell your skills in a matter of 10 to 15 critical seconds
- Make you sound like a strong candidate worthy of closer scrutiny
- Make that all-important first impression work for you, not against you

A resume features name and contact information, a skills summary (early in the resume), job history and education (order depends on the resume format you're using), and activities/awards (only those that pertain to your career field and illustrate your expertise).

Here are some general tips:

1. Put your strengths up front. Write a compelling "hook"—the summary statement or qualifications summary or skills summary (see chapter 2). These selling points carry the most weight of anything you have to say on the entire resume. Don't bury these at the end. Your goal is to knock 'em dead—not make the hiring manager have to figure out what you've done and why you think you're the right candidate for the job opening. This hook makes it clear what you have in the way of industry expertise. If you want to state a job objective, do so in your cover letter, where you refer to the specific position you're applying for.

2. If you're such a traditionalist that you can't resist listing an objective, which is definitely optional, tweak it to fit the position. A generic objective ("challenging position") won't score any points with a hiring manager.

3. Realize that a skills summary helps if you're one of these job seekers:
- You have an impressive set of skills.
- Your skills are more amazing than your jobs.
- Your skills are widely applicable—perfect for a number of different positions.
- You want to send your resume to multiple Internet data banks.

- Your resume format is reverse chronological order (see chapter 4).
- You're an executive or high-level candidate in your field. (You can call your skills summary an executive summary, if you want to.)

4. When you're deciding between using an objective or skills summary, keep in mind that most of today's recruiters and hiring managers find the skills summary more enticing. The objective is primarily a remnant of yesteryear.

What's the difference? Your job objective would be something of this order: Managing Editor of a regional magazine. For the same job, a skills summary would read: Professional journalist with ten years' experience, including writing, copyediting, proofreading, story tracking, and teaming. Known for excellence in meeting deadlines, organizing staff efforts, and uniting staffers in prioritized activities and extreme creativity.

Simply put, a skills summary supplies more information on your strengths than an objective does, and hiring managers scrutinize skills and experience as the chief elements of your resume. Don't make pivotal people dig!

5. To write a good skills summary (also known as an asset statement, skills statement, keyword profile, summary profile or qualifications summary), fill in the blanks of the following "skeleton" form:

Based on ___ years in _____(architecture, journalism, banking etc.), <u>seasoned</u> (or young or high-energy) professional seeks position that allows use of _____ skills (team-building, strong closing, creativity, etc.) to improve company's bottom line, strengthen overall effort, and deliver excellent <u>(product or service or technical expertise)</u>.

You can come up with your skills statements by thinking about your jobs and jotting down all the things you did. For example, someone with three years' experience as a medical receptionist may have answered phones, assisted the office manager, handled vendor requests, called patients who had office consultations but never scheduled surgery, sent letters to patients answering questions, sent flowers to patients who were recovering from surgery, sent out patient-satisfaction checklists, and more. Perhaps this was the receptionist's first and only job, but he can list that his skills include: ingenuity (he came up with the idea of the patient checklist), image-building (he calmed patients who had concerns), and multitasking (besides phone-answering, he had other responsibilities that increased during three years on the job, resulting in a promotion). So, based on what he has done and how these skills add up, his skills summary might go like this:

Based on three years in medical office administration, high-energy clerical professional seeks position that allows use of ingenuity, image-building, efficiency, and multitasking, to improve the bottom line and strengthen overall effort.

6. Include an objective only if it will help your cause. An objective may work to your advantage if one of the below describes where you are in your career:

- Brand-new graduate
- Career crossover person (you've worked as an attorney and now you want to be a college professor, for example)
- Job hunter who wants a certain position listed in a job bank (some sites that give you exposure to thousands of jobs a year are: www.hotjobs.com, www.topjobsusa.com, www.usajobs.opm.gov, www.monster.com, www.careerpath.com, and www.helpwanted.com)
- Multifaceted individual whose job history is so confusing it's hard for the resume-reader to figure out what kind of job you want

7. If you do include an objective, make it sizzle. Say what you want to do, why you think you would be a good person to hire, and examples of why you have been a well-regarded employee in the past.

Example: A position as a sales/office professional that capitalizes on expertise in developing accounts and maintaining them, and using strong sales skills to improve company's bottom line. Top producer with excellent track record of developing rapport with clients, closing sales, and surpassing sales quotas. Profitability improvement accomplished consistently via hard-hitting work ethic, organized goal-setting, and outgoing personality.

8.

Understand that some employers don't like objectives at the top of resumes because they interpret these as nothing more than a job candidate recycling what he read in the want ad.

9.

As applicable, include these basic elements in your resume: name (top line), contact information, summary of skills, education and training, job history (experience), activities and organizations, honors and awards. Note that you don't see a section marked "personal."

10. Include a section called "competencies" if you have some that are substantial. But don't use this title if you're talking about basics you know how to do, such as type and file, prepare food orders and serve tables, etc.

Examples of competencies are the following:

- Computer competencies: You should refer to computer programs and knowledge of the Internet. If you are a program administrator, programmer, etc., your areas of expertise may include: SQL Server, PowerPoint, MS Word, Outlook, software programming, network system engineering, Visual Basic, Windows 9X, XP, NT.

- Technical competencies: You have mastered the knowledge and skills that it takes to perform a certain job. For example, in public relations or marketing, you may be adept at developing market-share, servicing clients, planning PR campaigns, staging events, courting media contacts, working with nonprofits, etc.

- Leadership competencies: Also called core or behavioral competencies, these are the skills an executive needs to spearhead a corporate effort. A senior manager/supervisor may need to be a visionary, a strategic planner, a troubleshooter, a crisis-management expert, a communicator, etc.

11.

Lead with your best shot. If your education is stronger than your experience, put it first on your resume. If your experience is more impressive, list it before your education.

12.

Make sure that your resume is up-to-date. People often circulate resumes that don't include their most recent jobs and then tack on a little mention in the cover letter. This makes you look disorganized, and it doesn't motivate a hiring manager to take a chance on you. If you won't take the time to update your resume, why should a company representative assume that you would work hard to please a supervisor?

13.

Present the job candidate (you) in a favorable light. Ask an objective party to read your resume and tell you these things:

- Do you sound like someone with specific skills that can be used in the job you're applying for?
- Or does the resume wrongly emphasize skills and jobs that don't apply to the position you're seeking?

14. Make sure that you present yourself as a Sure Thing. Hiring you should present few or no risks to the hiring manager. Raise his comfort level with hiring you, even if you have never done this kind of work before.

15. Craft your resume to fit the position in the job listing and to target the particular company. (See chapter 11 for tips on customizing your resume.)

16. Make sure you understand what a hiring person in your desired profession wants to see in a resume. If necessary, contact someone who has a job in that field and ask to see his resume. For example, if you want to break into fashion design and you fail to mention on your resume that you have a portfolio, the person setting up interviews will know that you haven't done your homework, and probably won't let you get your foot in the door.

17. Do include unpaid jobs on your resume if they honed skills that are important in this particular job search. For example, if you want to be a day care worker, and you once did volunteer work at a children's shelter, feature this experience as a key element of your work history.

18. While you're accomplishing all of these things in your resume, don't make up information. No matter how much you would like to embellish the truth, don't do it. It's easy for human resource managers to verify information that you provide on a resume, so if you fib a bit, there's a good chance you'll get caught. You can't imagine a more embarrassing scenario. (And trying a new format doesn't give you license to glam up your resume with half-truths.) In these days of verification for everything, the truth will come out, and you don't want to tarnish your business reputation. No matter how little experience, or how irrelevant your experience is to the job you want, you can tweak a resume that will make you look and sound good. Go with the "reality show" of your true job history.

19. Play up any position you've held that has a touch of glitz or status to it, or one in which you worked for or with a "big name." Take advantage of star power. Hardly anyone is immune to being a bit starry-eyed when you mention that you were Julia Roberts's makeup artist or astronaut Neil Armstrong's speechwriter or President George Bush's inaugural ball photographer.

20. When you've finished your resume, check to make sure that you included the required information. Just because you don't like some element doesn't mean that you can "accidentally" leave it out. Perhaps you hate that you still live at home with your parents, and you'd rather not give the address (you know the interviewer will recognize a pricey neighborhood that no kid fresh out of college could possibly afford, so you must be living at home). You wonder: Won't I look like a ne'er-do-well if I'm still under my parents' roof when I'm twenty-five? The truth is, most employers are more interested in your skills and past jobs than the fact that you're a mama's boy, or a non-saver who can't seem to come up with the deposit for an apartment, or a clotheshorse who spends paychecks on being fashionable. Typically, the very things that you worry about on your resume—and wish you could simply leave out—aren't going to raise any eyebrows in the way that you might imagine.

21. Make your resume bold and clear. To employers, nothing is more impressive than a resume that resonates with clarity and confidence. Feature specifics of your work history that make you proud. These same things are likely to impress prospective employers. And don't include in your resume the parts of your life that you would rather cover or explain during an interview, such as having been incarcerated.

22.

Golden Rule of Resumes: If in doubt, leave it out. A popular Houston realtor tells of learning what to leave out when she was showing her first house early in her career, and she told the prospective buyer, "You can always change this awful shag carpet." The woman turned to the realtor and said, "I love shag carpet." No sale that day—but a good lesson in "less is more." If you keep going back and forth on a particular item you are considering putting in your resume, but a gut feeling tells you that it could give someone a poor impression of you, just don't include it (of course, only if it's an optional inclusion—not something that absolutely must be in a resume).

23.

Forget about trying to convey your personality in a resume. If that's important to you, show your vivaciousness in your cover letter, but tone down your resume so that it's a businesslike piece of communication. Don't overwrite. You have no idea what kind of person is making the decision on who gets an interview, and you're certainly not privy to that person's prejudices, likes or dislikes, or mood swings. To level the playing field, keep your resume factual, professional, and as close to perfect as a resume can get.

24. Write your resume with the assumption that the recipient is not going to read your cover letter. You can't predict the fate of your cover letter, but you can be fairly sure the resume will get a look. For that reason, you don't want to bury important accomplishments or awards in your cover letter unless you also have them in your resume. Commonly, frantic hiring managers review a resume before they decide to read the cover letter.

25. Include all information that you think may spur a hirer to contact you to set up an interview. But don't sound desperate: "I need a job so bad—I've been out of work for years. My children are hungry. Please help!" Remember that hiring managers want employees who are in demand—not ones who are the least desirable of all the candidates out there.

26. Concentrate on refining the employment section of your resume. A hiring manager wants to see quickly if you have experience that's a good fit for the job slot that needs to be filled. Study the employment section critically. Pretend you are a hiring manager and ask yourself: Does this person adequately describe the scope of his duties? The person reviewing your resume shouldn't have to search for the information he needs to read.

27. Delineate specific job tasks. For example, if you were a booking agent for a modeling agency, some of your duties may have been: contacting models to schedule them; handling the PR aspect of agency/model continuity; serving as an agency rep for media companies who want a "cattle call" for photo shoots; keeping a computer log of appointments, cancellations, and re-bookings; and planning ad campaigns and marketing efforts to spread the word about model camps and classes. A hiring manager who is looking for a computer receptionist capable of multitasking may find the model agency booker's skills quite appropriate even though the two fields of work are miles apart in thrust. The point is, if you really take the time to sell yourself and your skills, you may be pleasantly surprised at the wide range of opportunities that come your way.

28. Check for anything in your resume that may make a hiring manager chuckle. Don't list your Eagle Scout award if you're forty-three, or your Homecoming Queen win in college if you're a fifty-year-old seeking a position as a school librarian. Go easy on personal information, heavy on professional. The hiring manager doesn't want to date you (hopefully); he wants to find out if your skills sync up with the job that needs to be filled.

29.

Feature your willingness to relocate near the top of your resume. If you know you are moving to a certain city, clearly state: "Relocating to Atlanta, Georgia, in May 2004." If you are ready to move just about anywhere if the job sounds right, specify this, too: "Ready to relocate anywhere in the U.S. or internationally." If you have certain locale preferences, it's fine to list those, too. But don't mention places you absolutely wouldn't go. The hiring manager may be hiring for Philadelphia, but he may have grown up in Baltimore, and he won't like it when you say "anyplace but boring Baltimore!"

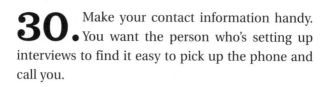

30.

Make your contact information handy. You want the person who's setting up interviews to find it easy to pick up the phone and call you.

31. If you've have found information on the company you want to work for (via the Internet or other research), allude to specifics about that company to show that you cared enough to do your homework. That shows two good points you can make about yourself—that you have ingenuity and that you're willing to put in the time it takes to get the job done well.

32. Check your resume with this question in mind: Did I spotlight what I bring to the table that will benefit this company? Example: If you have been a key player in increasing market-share growth for the company you now work for, be sure to include how you accomplished that and what skills and credentials you have that enabled you to pull off that feat.

33. Assess your resume with the "new realities" of today's business world in mind. Don't simply take the same route that you took twenty years ago when you were job hunting. Today, there are many more publications with job listings (not just your local newspaper), and you don't want to miss the online opportunities that can increase your chances of getting a job enormously. (See chapters 24 and 25 on e-resumes.) Also, you may want to send your resume in new directions. If you need to change your line of work in order to get a job, consider the fields that are hurting for employees, such as nursing, education, or the federal government.

34. Follow instructions listed in the job listing for presentation of the resume. If they ask you to mail it to a certain address, do that, and if they want an e-resume, prepare one as outlined in chapters 24 and 25. Don't improvise and decide to drop your resume by the office and ask to say hello to the hiring manager and chat a while. Hiring managers are very busy people, and your failing to observe boundaries will probably be viewed as a negative, not a positive.

35. Even if the job listing says nothing about a cover letter, include one! It is never wrong to top your resume with an excellent cover letter. (See chapter 21 for more on cover letters.) You could no more go wrong by including a cover letter than you could by sending an interview thank-you letter. Both are parts of the job hunt etiquette.

36.

Don't make the mistake of focusing on why you want the job instead of what you can do for the employer. The employer looks at your resume from his standpoint, as he should, and he expects you to anticipate that.

37. Don't send a bad signal by giving irrelevant information, such as describing your health problems or the poetry you've published. One hiring manager notes, "I assume that if you include irrelevant information in your resume and cover letter, if we hire you as a writer or editor, you would include irrelevant information in our career guides."

38. Remember that anything personal in your resume detracts unless it shows how you qualify for the position. In other words, if you want to be a rock star's bodyguard, the fact that you weigh three hundred pounds and have spent the past five years winning bodybuilding competitions is pertinent. But if you're applying for a job as a car salesman, don't include these tidbits of information.

39. Review your resume for problem areas and improve on anything that sounds vague. It you go for "generic," you probably will be bypassed for someone who sets out good reasons and evidence that he's interview-worthy and a good fit for the position.

40.
Assess the general "feel" of your resume. You want the hiring manager to get the impression that you are healthy, high-energy, innovative, and talented in your field. He should walk away from reviewing your resume with the idea that you are a keeper—the kind of employee who will be glad to get the job, will deliver the goods, and will be an asset (not a liability) as a supervisor, subordinate, or coworker.

2.

Make Your Irresistible Resume Flawless

No matter what resume approach you choose (see chapter 4), you must include certain vital pieces of information. You can vary style and form, but don't leave out the required (and expected) specifics about you and your work history that a prospective employer has every right to expect. Your goal is creating a resume as flawless as possible—one that has the "right stuff," presented attractively and neatly, and topped with a great cover letter (see chapter 21).

Some tips for a flawless resume are:

41. Provide complete and correct contact information. Include your email address, pager number, cell-phone number, home-phone number, mailing address, and website address (if you have one and the material on it is appropriate).

42. Don't include a long string of pager numbers or cell-phone numbers unless you want to broadcast your obsessive-compulsive nature. One of each is fine, but not three cell numbers, three pager numbers, etc.

43. Use your work number only if you have a direct line.

44. After your name and contact information, top your resume with your great hook—what your job search should lead to, or a skills summary.

45. Highlight your experience in a way that makes the most of what you have. Take a great deal of time in perfecting this section. You want to show off the skills that you have polished.

46.

For gaps in employment, show the year instead of the month and year. This makes your resume look more consistent.

47. Don't include a job title if it makes the job sound more menial or low-totem-pole than it actually was. While you may have been classified as secretarial assistant, your job may have branched into mini-management, bookkeeping, and public relations, so that means that you should not refer to the job merely as "secretarial assistant."

If your title on a certain job sounds really pathetic, choose another word to rename it. However, don't call yourself "computer team lead" if you were actually on a single committee. Just make your job as ad-agency receptionist sound a little better by calling yourself "interoffice coordinator." But that's only if you actually did serve as a coordinator of office activities at times (usually, receptionists perform a number of functions). Spicing up is OK; fabrication is not.

48. Don't include salary or bonus information. You can give a ballpark idea of the salary range in which you fall simply by listing job titles you have held. In other words, most people have a general idea what a legal secretary makes.

49. Don't list high school education if you have a college degree; it looks silly on a resume. List yourself as a high school graduate if you have a GED, but don't mention that it was a GED. In listing education, you start with your highest degree: type, your major, the college or university you attended, and the date your degree was awarded.

50. Do list your high-school education if your highest education beyond high school is completion of a vocational or tech school. If your education portion is slim, include courses, continuing education, conferences, seminars, and workshops you've completed, especially the ones that relate to the work you're pursuing.

51.

Present your education in the best possible light. Whether or not you have a degree (college), don't fail to include other extra courses that you have taken that weren't a part of a college or other higher-education regimen—but were perhaps continuing education, special workshops, seminars, and other growth opportunities. Even correspondence courses are worth mentioning.

52.
Feature accomplishments such as "improved workplace efficiency" and "increased sales" in place of Girl Scout of the Year, Prom Queen, or Alpha Tau Omega Sweetheart.

53.
Frame your activities/organizations section the right way. Highlight the parts that pertain to the kind of work you are going to do—but you don't want to include group associations that sound ridiculous or reveal your religious affiliations, political connections, and such. It's great that you were the president of the Young Republicans at Baylor University in Waco, Texas, but if the hiring manager is Bill Clinton's favorite cousin, you have the deck stacked against you before you ever have an opportunity to open your mouth at an interview.

54. Mention that you can provide clips of published writings/work samples/information and other pertinent-to-the-job items (such as videotape for broadcasting, license for an M.D., teaching certificate, etc.)

55. Flesh out parts of your resume that may raise questions. For example, if you're applying for a job as a hunting-lodge hunt leader, and you've been a hunter, you may want to establish where you stand on the hunting issue (took no trophies, used all hunt proceeds for food). Or maybe you think your application for a job as a receptionist will raise the question "Does he have computer skills?" Go ahead and include that information, just in case. Often, you can anticipate questions that will come up after a hiring manager peruses your resume.

56.
Include in your resume a mention of your license or certification required for the position (this is applicable to law, medicine, teaching, hairstyling, accounting, etc.). When asked to see your license during an interview, or prior to the interview, supply a copy. For obvious reasons, don't send off your only copy of your license!

57. Don't list your website address unless you have checked it for material that's not appropriate for a business viewing audience. Remember that photo of you and two friends cross-dressing? And that note from your best friend about your annoying tics?

58. After you put your phone number on your resume, immediately change your voice mail or answering machine message to one that sounds professional. Spooky, odd, or funny won't give the right impression.

59. List military experience as a separate section or as part of your work history. Include awards that you were given in the military, and tout skills you honed via military training.

60. Make your resume long if it's an international resume. Send in a one- or two-pager (the norm for a U.S. resume) and many international employers will mistake you for inexperienced, disinterested, or unmotivated. For them, the ideal resume is six to eight pages long and jam-packed with qualifications and experience. Use a chronological or combination resume for sending to international firms. On the first page, give a one-page summation of what will follow on the other pages—highlight the key points. In the international resume, you can ignore all the rules in this book about laying low on honors and awards unless they are extremely pertinent. The length of the international resume (often called a curriculum vitae) gives you room to provide names of awards, what they meant, why you got them, and pretty much everything else that you think will sell you as a candidate. Even personal information is often considered fine for inclusion.

61.

For federal jobs, use the federally formatted resume. Read the federal vacancy announcement, and follow the instructions for application. If you want help developing a strong resume for a federal job, see the website for Career Marketing Techniques on the Internet. (Email them at newcareer@polishedresumes.com; see www.polishedresumes.com.)

62. Do yourself justice. Sometimes a person applying for a job will leave out a part-time job that may be the very thing that would interest the person who is glancing over resumes for a certain position. An example: While waiting to find a job in her field, one sales professional worked part-time for a local author. She had never included the job on her resume because the skills she used (networking, serving as liaison with media outlets) were things that she had not used on sales jobs. However, when she added this item to her resume and sent out these resumes, she immediately got calls for interviews. Try to take a global view of what might be a turn-on to a human resources exec.

63. Don't include salary information for past jobs. Why divulge information that could earn you a lower salary offer than you might have gotten otherwise? If you have to fill out an application, in addition to submitting a resume, there will be a blank for "salary requirements," and you can put a range ($100,000 to $150,000).

64. On an application, when salary history is requested, you can put the base salary along with your commissions...but you can't lump in the amount that benefits add to the package.

65. Include a criminal record on your application form only and then only if you have not been able to get it expunged. It does not belong on your resume.

66. Don't draw attention to periods of unemployment by pointing out that you received unemployment compensation—a red flag to some employers. If asked, however, be honest during a phone call or in-person interview.

67. Make sure that you include concrete image-building information in your resume. If you have failed to present yourself as a desirable candidate, go back to the drawing board. Leaving out the boastful part of your resume is as bad as forgetting to include your phone number!

68. Include hard skills in your resume. Hard skills are the nitty-gritty tangibles, such as using computer skills, supervising employees, and preparing reports. For each concrete "hard" skill, list something you did that shows you have this skill.

Example: Demonstrated top skills in fundraising, which were widely copied, and admired, and drew a request from a publisher for a fundraising book (written in 2000 and published in 2001).

69. Include soft skills, too. Soft skills are the intangible ones that are harder to quantify yet still very important to many employers; examples are team spirit, gregarious personality, dependability, etc. Don't overdo this stuff because listing soft skills ad nauseam can quickly start to sound self-serving.

70. Don't include your marital status—married, separated, divorced, widowed, or single, or your number of children, the fact that you have no children, or that you're pregnant. Never list height, weight, hair or eye color—unless you're seeking a job in acting, modeling, or some other field that merits a physical description.

71. Do mention the positions of your superiors if you're sure that those carry weight. In other words, if you were an assistant to the CEO of the company, it's mention-worthy, but if you were an assistant to the assistant stockman in charge of stocking shelves, maybe not.

72. In special fields that call for interning or student training (such as student teaching for teachers), include the practice period on your resume as proof of your learning-the-ropes period. The way in which you paid your dues—and the things you learned—are definitely pertinent enough to feature in a resume.

73. Show that you're not just computer-literate but also computer-hip. Include recent computer skills such as Oracle, SAP, Microsoft Excel, Word, Access, etc. But don't list COBOL, Fortran, and other outdated computer skills.

74.

Flaunt language skills. If you speak a foreign language, absolutely give yourself credit. List your skill level: read/write, beginning, intermediate, fluent. But don't misrepresent your skill level because this can be verified easily.

75. Don't attach letters of recommendation, a list of references, or copies of your licenses and certifications. Wait until a potential employer asks to see these things.

76. Remember that your resume is only one part of a major portfolio that is expected in certain fields, such as interior design, wedding planning, fashion design, graphic design, photography, advertising, public relations, or journalism. For example, the journalist who has no "clips" will have a difficult time getting a job in the field of journalism. (Clips are examples of stories, articles, and features that have been published with your byline. Lacking these, include stories you wrote in college; choose the ones with a big, fat A at the top.)

3.

Wow Them With Words

Resumes are all about—what else?—words. That means, of course, that choosing the right words is one way to make sure that your quest for an interview gets a thumbs-up, especially when a harried human resources director is hurriedly flipping through stacks of resumes for the very job you would kill to have.

The following tips tell you how to wow them with words:

77.

Use verb phrases to describe what you've done on your various jobs. This is one time when complete sentences are incorrect.

Examples: Created teaming workshops that improved company morale. Led training sessions to enhance new employees' formatting skills. Demonstrated project skills that were so noteworthy they won numerous awards.

78. Follow typical resume telegraphic style, which calls for minimal use of articles (a, an, the) and omission of the words "I" and "me." Avoid entirely the use of first person. Wrong: "I worked three years in financial analysis, and I was promoted to senior financial analyst." Instead, say: "Worked three years in financial analysis; promoted to senior financial analyst."

79. Don't write a resume in narrative fashion: "And then the company decided to hire two managers, and after that, they went on to set up a program…."

80. Use active voice rather than passive voice.

Example: Supervised fifteen employees. Wrong: Fifteen employees were supervised by me.

81. Check for jargon that makes you sound like you're auditioning for a gang, a boy band, or the *Jerry Springer Show*. Buzzwords for corporate America go in and out very fast, so if you're still mired in terms like *proactive* and *self-motivated*, it's time to read some trade journals and spiff up your industry lingo. Words that sounded cool three years ago may be passé by now. Better to use none than to kill your chances with archaic or regional dialect: A cover letter that says you were "fixing to" work on your MBA will rate chuckles almost anywhere in the U.S. except the Deep South, where that phrase is used.

82.

Steer clear of the expression "was responsible for" because that's a negative hot button for many hiring managers. Why? Simple. It doesn't tell anyone the critical issue about responsibilities: Did you pull them off with flair? Were your efforts commendable or lukewarm? Did you win the kudos of management or did you lose your job?

83. Check for consistency in use of numbers (in other words, if you've used numerals in one place for a dollar amount, use them elsewhere, too).

84. In listing your computer experience (if you have some), be sure to spell and capitalize correctly company names and software programs. Example: Microsoft Word is two words, but WordPerfect is run together, with no space between Word and Perfect. The same is true of Page-Maker. Getting these things right shows attention to detail.

85. Understand the deficiency of a spellchecker. If you use an incorrect word—such as your for you're—a computer won't catch a word used in the wrong way.

86. Don't use British spellings—and don't use British pronunciations in your interview, either. One interviewer tells of a big burly Oklahoma guy applying for a coaching job who said he would have to check his "shedyule," using the British pronunciation, and the interviewer found this so odd that he didn't hire the man. Don't set yourself apart as an oddball by trying to seem unique.

87. Use words that provide insight into the kind of employee you are. Eternally, supervisors, human resources directors, and headhunters worry that a new employee will turn out to be difficult, lazy, gossipy, whiney, or tardy. Thus, you may want to point out in your resume or cover letter that you are an innovative, conscientious self-starter who stays calm under pressure, meets deadlines, and is a team player eager to learn (or whatever your own assets happen to be).

88. Do not use "shy" language when it comes to describing your strengths. Think of the things that past supervisors have liked about you, and play up those attributes big time.

Example: Spearheaded a multimillion-dollar project to completion by being the negotiator/leader between the art and editorial departments.

89.

Keep a lid on your inner comedian when you are writing. A resume is no time to be funny.

90. Describe your skills and experiences so that they sound noteworthy enough to interest the decision-maker; try to put yourself in his place and decide if you would grant an interview on the basis of this resume. Tout yourself!

91. Spotlight instances in which your ideas were implemented, but also prove the success by citing percentage of market share gained, or the amount of money made, instead of just stating "everyone loved the project." (That is like being a writer and saying your mother loved your book.) Give concrete evidence in numbers and dollars to show that your bright idea was successful. Here, the wording is extremely important. If you don't have numbers and dollars to brag about, use other specifics, such as "Christmas ad campaign ideas were implemented for three consecutive years."

92. Incorporate keywords/buzzwords reflective of the particular industry/profession to accommodate resume scanning. When a headhunter looks online for a candidate for a certain job, he may do a search of resumes in hopes of finding job-hunting individuals whose resumes happen to have keywords such as "corporate leadership" or "team building" or "business development."

Keywords can be a make-or-break factor in your job search (chapters 24 and 25 explain resume scanning). Some companies automatically funnel all resumes through a human resources department, where they are scanned visually or by computer, which results in some excellent resumes inadvertently getting excluded if someone fails to see the markers of good skills in a complex profession (like engineering). "As a result, they forward to the department supervisor resumes of unqualified candidates and toss some resumes of good candidates we would like to hire," explains one chemical engineer who has seen this happen.

To show you how it works, here are some job areas and a few appropriate keywords to blast into your resume:

- Supervisor, manager, administrator: crisis management, teaming, project management, bachelor's degree, office manager, personnel development, production schedule, data analysis, team-building, organizational structure
- Journalist, artist, creatives: idea-driven, deadline-oriented, creative, talented, bachelor's degree, art school, copy writing, editing, visionary
- Financial planner, stockbroker: portfolio management, damage control
- Info techie: support services, help desk, end user support, systems configuration, rightsizing
- Engineer: design, construction, project, project management, project engineer, process, process engineer, control system, control engineer, mechanical, civil, chemical, structural, instrumentation, bachelor of science

- Human resources professional, recruiter: bachelor of science, business administration, diversity training, leadership development, teaming, recruiting, staffing, wage-and-salary administration
- Salesperson: client list, motivated, strong closer, goal-directed, sales manager, sales director, top producer, client grooming, follow-up

93. Keep in mind that you are using the power of persuasion to finagle an interview. For example, you must convince the person who is handing out interview slots that your ten-year history as a reporter for the *Houston Chronicle* is an excellent match for *Philadelphia* magazine's need for "a seasoned journalist capable of taking on a variety of assignments and working with little supervision." Persuasive line: "Experienced reporter with varied writing repertoire, excellent multitasking ability, and topnotch initiative."

94. Avoid language that sounds flowery or condescending.

95. Don't be wordy. Instead of writing, "was responsible for the implementation of a new database system," use "implemented new database."

96. Opt for powerful verbs that convey your strengths effectively.

Examples are: boosted, chaired, created, demonstrated, devised, directed, developed, envisioned, established, expedited, facilitated, instituted, inspired, led, negotiated, organized, maximized, mentored, modernized, motivated, pioneered, prioritized, promoted, redirected, rerouted, revamped, spearheaded, streamlined, strengthened, upgraded.

97. Make your resume words energetic enough to intrigue the interview appointment-maker. Use "hot" words such as *contributed, created, produced, facilitated, engineered* instead of more anemic words such as *gave, set up, made, helped, planned.*

98.

Showcase your innovative benchmark moments by using very specific word pictures: If you're a manager, for example, don't just say "generated sales with rewards," say "awarded top producers one-year health-club memberships." If you're a receptionist, don't say "job description expanded during tenure," say "office manager expanded job description in recognition of extra skills and abilities evidenced in everyday performance excellence."

99. Resist the time-crunch temptation of making your resume generic in word or tone, as if you're trying to make it widely applicable for many different positions and companies. Instead, use power words to provide a dynamic and attractive sketch of your work background and exactly what makes you a standout (for the eyes of the potential employer you are wooing). Be scrupulously truthful, but take care to present yourself in a way that makes your work record sizzle.

100. Choose your words carefully when describing how your skills mesh perfectly with the position requirements in the job listing; no part of your resume matters more.

101. Avoid generalities: If you are simply telling an employer (generically) that you want "a challenging opportunity," you are actually saying absolutely nothing.

102. Make your resume lively and interesting. Use a tone that is upbeat and reflects a can-do employee.

Example: "Experienced and enthusiastic actor ready to take on new functions in theatre and willing to exhibit flexibility in audition hours and opportunities."

103. Make sure that you can live up to your description of job responsibilities that you claim you can handle. For example, if you list on your resume that you have experience in sales, that sends the message to the employer that you know how to develop new business, that you understand customer service, that you are a strong closer, and so on.

104. Do not use poetry in your resume, please. (We're glad you know how to write poetry, but poems won't do you any favors in a job search.)

105. Double-check to see that you have worded your resume in a way that leaves a single strong impression—that you are a candidate who would make a valuable employee.

106. Check for instances of words that are too boastful or pretentious.
    Examples: "Best employee your company has ever hired." Or: "Top real-estate salesperson in the country."

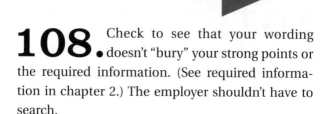

107.

Avoid words that make you sound frivolous.
   Example: "Cute fashionista looking for job as receptionist in classy office."

108. Check to see that your wording doesn't "bury" your strong points or the required information. (See required information in chapter 2.) The employer shouldn't have to search.

109. Review your resume for brevity and effectiveness. You want it to seem deceptively simple even though it takes writing/ editing/proofreading to produce.

110. Prune. Go back over your resume and see where you have used two sentences when one would suffice.

111.

Check for telltale signs of bitterness (about past jobs), backbiting (about coworkers), self-righteousness (about promotions not granted), and arrogance (about skills). Any of these signals will be the kiss of death for that interview you want.

112.

Check your finished resume for specifics. Strengths are most powerfully communicated quantified as accomplishments: "Saved $1 million annually by realigning operational areas." Tell how your success in giving an appealing corporate presence to widgets, and raising profits 15 percent, proves that you have a noteworthy marketing background.

113.

Put your resume aside for an hour or so, and then pick it up again to see how it reads cold. Go over your resume several times. Ask a friend or relative to proof it, too. Have a zero-tolerance policy toward mistakes. You absolutely do need to "fix" that missing period and the excess space between words in a sentence. You don't want to give the impression that mediocre or close-to-right is plenty good enough for you.

114. Review the language you have used by applying this yardstick: You want the management person to read about you and fear that letting you get away would be a big mistake. Good inclusions: "Promoted three times in three years," or "Received the highest number of accolades from customers for two consecutive quarters." Or if you don't have any big coups, say something low-key, like "Received praise from supervisor for meeting deadlines consistently."

115.
Make sure that every sentence reinforces the key point—*that you bring value to the company.*

4.

Choose the Perfect Format

Your resume is the primary marketing tool for your job search. It may be your only representative in the front line, and because you can't actually introduce yourself, you have to make it speak for you. It should express your energy, courage, and tenacity, the self-promotion skills that will make you stand out from the crowd. Wherever you are in your career, there's a resume format that's right for you. If you are fresh out of school, if you've had ten jobs in five years, or if you've worked thirty years at the same company, choosing the right resume format is the most important way to show off your unique skills.

Here are tips on finding and using the best format for your resume:

116. Modularize to facilitate e-resume modification. A resume's modules are: Name; Contact Information; Keyword Summary; Skills Summary and/or Summary of Professional Experience; Technical Skills; Professional Experience; Accomplishments; Duties and Responsibilities; Education; Honors, Awards, Activities. Each module is interchangeable, depending on the requirements of the position and your knowledge of the company and industry.

117. As you alter the format of your current resume, or write your very first resume, keep tabs on the balance. You want to sound like you're brimming over with confidence and smarts, but you don't want to come across as full of yourself or arrogant. Run your resume past the eyes of some friends who will give you their honest opinions.

118.
Understand that recruiters and hiring managers don't really like chronological resumes. They don't like having to weed through old jobs to get to the part they hunger for—your three to five years of recent job activity.

119. Use the reverse chronological resume if you want the most traditional, expected format. The reverse chronological type is the granddaddy of resume formats. Begin with most recent experience first, followed by each employer, ending with your first employer. This is the method most employers love because it shows where and when you acquired your skills.

120. Use the reverse chronological resume if you've had good job tenure, with little or no time in between jobs. This format works well for people who have had strong job continuity. If you don't have that asset, choose a format that doesn't highlight your spotty work record or long stretches of unemployment.

121. Write a functional resume if you want to list your skills, followed by employers—a good format if your skills are more impressive than the kinds of jobs you have had. Play up what you can do (organize, lead, sell, inspire) and play down the fact that you did these things at Burger King.

122. Use a functional resume if you've had many jobs in a short period of time or if you have a big gap in employment. A functional resume focuses on your job and industry skills and de-emphasizes tenure with employers.

123.
Try using the combination resume, which is a combo of the functional and reverse chronological formats. In the current days of scanning, both by computers and humans, the combination resume is useful for featuring a quickie list of functional skills, followed by a more in-depth listing (employer by employer).

124. Use the combination (mix-and-match) resume if you have had nice, long periods of employment on your jobs and a good employment history. Combination resumes have the elements of reverse chronological resumes as well as a skills listing, so you need good tenure and employment history for this kind of resume to serve you well.

125. On any format you choose, include functional skills—duties and responsibilities that you carry out in your daily business. This is the bedrock of resumes, one of the reasons you get hired.

Example: "Created monthly sales and marketing tracking logs."

126. On each format, include skills that reflect the industries you've worked in. This is especially important if you have worked in several different industries.

127. In each format, list your transferable skills. A skill that you learn from one employer and take to another employer is called "transferable." All skills are transferable, or you would have to work at the same place your entire life.

Skills transfer in various ways. In a vibrant economy, you can go from one job to another, using only your functional skills or industry skills for leverage. In a flat economy, at the management level, you probably will need both the functional and industry skills to compete.

128. On your resume, follow the hook with your experience unless you're a new graduate, in which case you follow the hook with your education.

129. In every type of format, don't be shy when you list your accomplishments. Your fellow job seeker won't be. Quantify your accomplishments: saved time, saved money, made time, made money. If you've been working five or more years, or if you have been in management, you will be hired based on your accomplishments more than on your ability to complete a task.

130.

Include plenty of examples of specific coups, such as "Saved the corporation $1 million by restructuring the business process and eliminating redundant steps."

131. Use the curriculum vitae (CV) format if you are in academia, medicine, or governmental positions. CV is a fancy word for a long, detailed resume—a type rarely used outside the realms of academia, medicine, or government. Essentially, CVs are like reverse chronological resumes on steroids. In writing a curriculum vitae, you go into long and explicit detail about each place of employment, and you focus on accomplishments, for example, "Discovered a new fountain of youth." CVs also include lists of publications, seminars, presentations, and honors.

In this day of identity theft, be careful what you include in your CV. In the past, doctors included license numbers and family members' names, but this is not advised, considering the possible problems inherent in such disclosures.

132. Another alternative is the letter format, which is less reader-friendly, but fits professions that post a job listing requesting a letter of self-introduction. (See chapter 21 for information on cover letters; you use the same form, but the letter format for resumes just includes more detailed information.) Try to include much the same information that you would put in a resume. Provide the essentials. However, don't make the letter longer than three pages even though it is a departure from the norm.

133. Present yourself in a skills-centered format if you're in a trade that focuses on drawing clientele because of your unique talents. (See chapters 4 and 9.) Examples are barber, hairstylist, fashion designer, wedding planner, personal trainer, etc.

134. Use an international format if you need a resume that will work worldwide and give you access to jobs in other countries.

135. When choosing a format, do a rough draft of the kind of resume you think showcases you best and then pass it to a peer or two for review and suggestions. Ideally, if you have a supervisor at your current job who is willing to keep your confidence, ask that individual to peruse your resume and assess the format. Having your resume reviewed by a discreet manager can be a big bonus.

136. Don't spend too much time deciding on or revising the format. Your resume is just a marketing tool solely designed to get you an interview. Do your best to produce an outstanding resume, but most important, get it done and send it out into the world. If you have a perfect resume but you wait six months to float it, you may have missed many good opportunities. Just do it!

137. Keep an open mind to criticism. If a prospective employer informs you that you are not using the right format, or a friend tells you that your resume is woefully inadequate, listen to them!

138.

Revise your resume in response to advice and requests for more information. Keep your resume cooking on the back burner, and experiment with new formats. Don't be afraid to be adventurous if your current resume isn't reaping interviews.

139. As you revamp your resume into a new-and-improved format, keep in mind that you need to make it work for you. Remember that you are competing with tens, hundreds, maybe thousands of other resumes for a thirty-second glance from the human resources person or the hiring manager. Make your resume sizzle! (See chapter 3 on choosing the right words.)

140. Somewhere in your newly formatted resume, include a summary statement—basically, a value-added summary of your skills and background. Example: 10+ years of progressive information technology management. Spearheaded ORACLE implementation that saved $3 million in two years. Focuses included LAN, WAN, ORACLE implementations. (See chapter 2 on the elements of a good resume.)

141. Avoid using a format commonly referred to as a "resume lite." Some career search doctrine advises that you send a capsule account of your resume as a teaser. The idea is that sending this "mini-resume" will prompt a phone call from the recipient, who will be eager to hear the rest of the story. Right? Wrong. Human resources departments and hiring managers move at the speed of light nowadays. If they don't get your story in the first thirty seconds, they are not going to call you for the rest. You have a very small window of opportunity, and it is important to seize it.

142.

In every type of format except the letter, you can use bullets, which are popular ways to shoot the reader short, pithy sentences. Bulleted information is easy to read, and in the age of warp-speed resume gulping, you need to grab attention fast. (See more on bullets in chapter 5.)

143.

If you don't want to use bullets, blocks of paragraphs work if you have a concentrated amount of experience that needs to be grouped together. Be careful not to make your paragraphs any longer than six lines, and break paragraphs up with spaces so that you have plenty of white space on your resume. Don't include a big, solid block of text; no one will read that. If you do use block paragraphs in your resume, make sure that the paragraphs are short and separated by a line. This gives the reader's eye a starting point and a stopping point.

144. For every format except the curriculum vitae (CV), you must get your resume message across in one to two pages. You are generally hired on the basis of your most recent three to five years of experience, so you need to highlight that period. Shorten your previous experience and fit the essentials on two pages.

5.

Make Your Resume Look Polished

The organization and look of your resume are direct reflections on you. Many employers say that a clear, concise resume will not only get more attention, it is more likely to get the candidate hired. Remember that a resume is not necessarily ready to go just because you have dotted your i's and crossed your t's, spell-checked, and grammar-checked. The format and look of your resume are important, too. Once you declare your resume "well-written," you must choose a typeface, type size, and look. There are some very specific guidelines for this, and not much wiggle room in the rule book.

Note: The advice in this chapter applies to hard-copy resumes. For the rules on e-resumes, see chapter 25.

Consider the following tips on the look and feel of your resume:

145. Consider magazine style. Magazines and some websites are enticing because trained professionals have taken the time to design documents that are easy to read and draw your eye around the document. Magazines use fonts, photos, and placement to catch your eye. So do websites. Since you can't include photos, work with fonts, bullets, and placement.

146. Strut your best right up front. Rearrange if necessary. Remember that item number one will be considered more important than item number six. Accomplishments such as saved money, made money, or saved time are job skills that employers admire, so make sure these assets are prominently displayed.

147. Make your resume no more than two pages long. Extend it onto a third page only if you absolutely have to. To compress the material, you can delete details from older positions and just list the company, position, and dates.

148. Be consistent. The style should remain the same from page one to two, from top to bottom. Don't change type styles or sizes within. (You would be surprised how often employers receive resumes that contain a number of typefaces and sizes within the single document.)

149.

Use uniform margins of at least one inch. Anything less will give your resume a very gray, off-putting look.

150. Let your line spacing be a good indicator of your consistency as an employee. For example, if you separate the Skills section from the Work Experience section with a double space, then you should do this between other sections of the resume. A look of inconsistency sends the message that you are inconsistent. The fact that this may not be a true reflection of you as an employee doesn't count if that is how the interviewer perceives you.

151. Get the tiny things right. For example, a dash (em dash) should not have spaces before or after it. Similarly, if you're using no periods in your degree (BA instead of B.A.), make sure you are consistent and do the same thing anywhere else your degree is mentioned. If you've listed the city and state where you held a job as Channelview, TX, be sure you use the same form for other jobs you list—a state abbreviation rather than spelled out.

If you are a medical doctor, place the M.D. after your name—Major Healer, M.D., not Dr. Major Healer. Also, don't put Dr. Major Healer, M.D., which is like saying "doctor, doctor."

152. Make sure that the material you indent aligns vertically, or the visual zigzags can be disconcerting. Set tabs to ensure that you are getting this right.

153. Make the dates of your jobs flush-right or flush-left.

154. Don't use underlining.

155. Use italics sparingly. These are hard to read, but you'll need them if you mention the name of a magazine, book, play, or boat/ship.

156.
Make your resume dynamic without sending along a "prop," such as a Pez dispenser emblazoned with your name, or a toy-phone receiver with your picture on it.

157. Do not include artwork borders. Resumes need to be more sedate than most room interiors. Avoid making the resume decorative in any way; straightforward is best. Use no clip art—keep it plain and simple.

158. Don't use colored paper. When you mail out resumes, chartreuse will not make the difference between its being read or ending up in the shredder. It may get your resume noticed, but not in the way you want. Hiring managers consider it unprofessional to use a resume shade other than white, natural white, off white, ivory, or gray. No pinks, blues, etc. Applying for a job in an artistic area is the exception.

159. If your dream job is theater, public relations, or an ad agency, you can go out on a limb and do something like put your resume inside a pizza delivery box. That will get you noticed. Someone will look at your resume. Then again, it never hurts to stick with the basics.

160. Remember that your cover letter stationery and your resume don't have to match. This is often asked. Unless you're applying to work for a stickler like Martha Stewart, you can have cover letter stationery that's different from your resume. The reader probably won't care one way or the other because he's looking for substance, not color coordination. The key to getting your resume out there is to send it. Don't worry if it doesn't match.

161. Avoid fancy fonts. Use Arial or Times New Roman, something simple and common. Since you have to cut-and-paste your resume to apply for jobs online, you should be aware that some programs turn your pristine resume into gobbledygook. Remember, the goal is a resume that's a snap to read and understand. Many experts recommend a serif type over one that is sans-serif, based on the belief that serif is simply easier to read. Times New Roman is serif and Arial is sans-serif.

162. Use a standard font size. Standard font sizes are 10, 11, or 12 point. You won't make a short resume look meatier by trying to spread it all over the page by using huge fonts. The reader will figure that one out. By the same token, if you have a long resume, don't try to cram it all on one or two pages by using a microscopic font. If your resume is longer than two pages, omit the details from earlier positions. List the bare bones for those positions: Company, City, Dates, and Position Title.

163. In the business world, employers hire you based on your most recent three to five years of work experience. Government and academia will go farther back into your professional history, but business has a short look-back period. So if your goal is a job in the business world, don't bother including details of positions that are not going to be considered in the hiring process.

164. Don't use gigantic bullets or tiny ones—use the in-between size.

165. Don't try to be e.e. cummings and send a resume with no caps whatsoever. It worked for him because he was a poet; it won't work for you in your job search. They will just brand you "weird."

166. Never submit your resume or curriculum vitae as a zip file. No one wants to open one of these gargantuan things.

167. Avoid using fancy graphics because these annoy most hiring managers. (The exception would be if you apply for a job in an arts field, which allows more leeway. For information on these resumes, see chapter 9.)

168.
Don't draw pictures in the margin. One recruiter tells of receiving a resume in which the person listed "migraine headaches" under the personal section, and then sketched drawings of a man with his hands holding his aching head all over the margins of the resume. What was he *thinking*?

169. Check for wrinkles and smudges before you mail that resume. If a hiring manager gets a dingy-looking resume, he will assume that you could be as bad at the job as you are at self-promotion.

170. Check these things: Do your skills stand out? Is it easy to find the different sections quickly? Does it look *au courant*?

171. Avoid single-spacing your resume. A resume with only single spacing is a real snoozefest. If your resume is so crammed and jammed that it reminds you of your Granny's knick-knack shelves, pare down. If you compacted it in order to get more information on the page, you will simply have to do some judicious editing and weed out items that you're not in love with.

172. Use white space. Avoid a document that's solid text, no breathing space, and just a solid, dark bank of words. To make sure your resume gets read, which really increases your chance of getting an interview and getting hired, feature nice blocks of text, with white space in between. You can play with the margin of the document to get your information on the page.

173. Feature your contact information prominently but not gaudily. Include your name, address, telephone, cell phone, and email address. Make it easy for hiring managers to contact you. Have your contact information clearly visible on your cover letter and the first page of your resume at the top.

174. Don't put a picture in the envelope with your resume. Yes, you may be exceptionally cute, but still—no photos, please. Sending your photo with your resume went out in the sixties—yes, 1960s. Why? For one reason, the Civil Rights Act of 1967 set guidelines to end discrimination against women, minorities, and other protected groups. A sure way to tell if a candidate is female or a minority is to see a picture. This means that employers prefer not to get a picture of you because they want to decide whether or not to interview you based solely on your qualifications.

175. Forget the bells and whistles and confetti. Cheesy is bad. Anything you put in the envelope that might make you seem silly probably isn't a great idea. When in doubt, leave it out.

176.

Use all-caps for headers only, if you use them at all: PROFESSIONAL EXPERIENCE, EDUCATION, etc.

177.

Make sure to number subsequent pages if your resume is more than one page and label the second page with your name, too. (Assume that the resumes could get dropped on the floor and someone will have to scoop them up and put them back together.) Include this information on the top left-hand side of subsequent pages:

Kay Rotterdam

Page 2

6.

The Virgin Resumes

You may have avoided writing a resume until now because of fear and anxiety. After all, being at the very beginning of your career can make tackling a resume daunting. You may feel nervous because you're a new high school or college grad with little or no experience—someone who truly wants to go to work but can't find much to put on a resume. Essentially, the best way to get a good job when you graduate is to make good grades at a good school, be active on campus and in the community, hold leadership positions, have a major in a discipline that's marketable, and show signs of a strong work ethic and good attitude.

Here are tips for a new graduate who wants to write a resume:

178.
Discover your strengths and find a type of work in which you can capitalize on them. If you're not sure what your strengths are, take an aptitude test and ask friends and family for their opinions. Once you do know your strengths, feature these prominently on your resume.

179.
Take advantage of the resume resources available to you. Many schools, colleges, and universities offer workshops and seminars on resume writing. Also, don't forget to tap the vast knowledge of your school counselor or career advisor, who often know what hiring managers want to see on resumes.

180. Study a job listing for some of the attributes you can mention (that you have) that are as good or better than the hiring requirement (one you don't have). Perhaps you want to go to work in hotel management, and your bachelor's degree in biology seems like a stretch. But you can pole-vault over any misgivings the hiring manager may have by pointing out that you gained experience in dealing with people when you served as a biology lab assistant; it was a demanding job, and you won praise for your people skills. (Don't say that you qualify because you've stayed in lots of hotels unless you're trying to get a job as the hotel's stand-up comic.)

181. Keep in mind that you, a new grad, will be hired for your potential and your academic achievements. Also of importance are your internships and summer jobs that are in your field of study and exposed you to the profession hands-on.

182.

"Dance with who brung you." It's an old quote from a popular Texas football coach who was basically saying that a person should try to make the best of what he has. In the case of a new graduate, this means scratching your head hard to think of things you've done that translate into resume plusses. For example, let's say that you're a recent high school grad who covets a recreation director job at the local community center, but no one seems to think you're old enough or qualified. You can list on your resume the "summer job" you had as a kid when you gathered all the little kids in your neighborhood and taught them reading, writing, dance, and song. The parents loved you for being an unpaid day care center. The kids loved you because you so obviously enjoyed them. Translate this small coup into the following on your resume:

> Summer Recreation Leader: Instructed children ages five to seven in reading, writing, and dance. Won the praise of parents for initiative, sense of humor, and organizational skills.

183. Be creative. When the door keeps slamming in your face after the hiring managers have said, "Come back to see us when you have some experience," it's time to sit down at the computer and list all the reasons that the employer would be glad he hired you. Make the reasons applicable to the particular job. Be convincing. Make your words compelling. Your sincerity and creativity just may get you an interview—and, if you're lucky, the job.

184.
As a new grad, don't hesitate to exploit the high-energy aspects of employing you. Youth, good health, and individual-with-no-children are assets that you bring to the table. You don't have to denigrate fellow job-seekers to make yourself look good ("I'm better than that creepy old guy I just saw you interviewing") but you can single out the things that set you apart when you're a young, fresh job-hunter and make those qualities have the ring of true job assets.

185. Use reverse chronological order (see chapter 4 on formats).

186. List academic appointments, scholarships, chairs, and offices held, in the activities section.

187. Include your GPA only if it's high—3.0 or better. If you decide to list the GPA you posted when you took courses in your major, that's fine—but you must indicate that's what you are doing; don't try to fudge. Saying that you had a 4.0 when that was only in your major field isn't being honest if your overall GPA was 2.7, for example.

188.

Don't send a big, fat package. Don't attach things to your resume: no book reports, papers, report covers, blue books, transcripts, or letters of recommendation. Of course, the exception to this is when a hiring manager specifically asks you to include one of these things.

189. As a workplace virgin, you can have a summary of skills, or a professional summary—or not. If you have had any jobs during your school years, summarize the skills you gained or improved upon. Highlight your skills. (Also, in the current days of scanning of resumes, this gives you another chance to insert keywords that might be critical in having your resume selected for review.)

190. Write different resumes to target different jobs. You just got out of school, so you should have lots of energy and a recent memory of "the right way" to write—clearly and succinctly.

191.
Be sure to include any technical skills you learned in high school or college, if these are pertinent to the job you want.

192. Use your sports background to show that you're a team player. And if your resume is very skimpy, list the teams you were on: soccer team (MVP two years), softball team captain, tennis club singles champ, etc.

193. Mention your science fair project ribbons and research paper successes only if you've just graduated from high school.

194. Place your "work experience" section carefully. This depends on your years of experience. If you are a new graduate, list your education before your work experience. You are being hired mainly for your grades, the university you attended, and your activities during university. But if you have been out of school more than five years, list your education after your work experience.

195. If you're a young woman, don't broadcast that you plan to try to "start a family" in the next few years even if it's true. You want an employer to invest a great deal of money in training you, and talking about when you plan to leave to have a baby is no way to ingratiate yourself.

196. Write a resume that maximizes the advantages that come with being a brand-new grad. In other words, you want to take what some people may consider a huge downside (no or little experience) and turn it into a great big advantage. Emphasize that you're hip; you have knowledge and skills that resonate; you are fresh out of college and on the cutting edge of the industry (whatever industry it happens to be). For example, if you're a new teacher, you are up-to-date on educational trends; you know all about security measures in today's schools; you understand the handling of gender-prejudice issues and sex-bias lawsuits; you know how to prepare lesson plans and deliver classes that will ensure your students acquire the knowledge needed to pass current national/state proficiency tests.

197. Emphasize the blank-slate aspect of being a new graduate. Somewhere in your resume or cover letter, find a way to play up the advantages inherent in hiring a person with no preconceived notions or baggage in the working world. You are open to new ideas. You won't ever keep harking back to "the way we used to do it on my last job." You are a blank slate ready to be imprinted with your first employer's way of doing things, preferences, and priorities.

198. Study your profession's hot buttons, and make sure you play these up in your resume.

199.

Consider the skills that older people in the profession may lack (computer savvy, for example) and emphasize the point that you learned all of this and much more in college. Be specific about the programs you are well versed in using.

200. Include everything you can to make yourself sound like a real catch. Even though you lack real-world experience, the company supervisor who is smart enough to hire you may be patting himself on the back in a few years.

201. Stay focused and realistic. In your summary statement, don't get too elaborate or pompous. You can say: Seeking a position in the food-service industry that will provide workplace experience in a team atmosphere. Don't say: Seeking a highly exhilarating and challenging position in food service that will enable me to illustrate my outstanding burger-prep skills and that will have excellent potential for upward mobility and fair remuneration.

202.

Don't go overboard when emphasizing how much a new grad knows versus a graduate of 1984. Your interviewer may be a 1984 grad who may mistake your enthusiasm for arrogance.

203.

Use the concept of "stretch." Expand on something as simple as an internship to make it look like more than it probably actually was. While the hiring manager is not exactly fooled, she will still like your ingenuity in maximizing the things you have had a chance to do so far.

204.

If you're a graduate who has never had a job or internship, and your grades aren't anything to brag about, play up your education. If you helped out in the attendance office, use that. If you were given detention so many times that the teacher made you his deputy assistant, use the assistant part (and don't mention that you were the Queen of Tardy). If you took a photojournalism class that you enjoyed, talk about the photographs you took that were used in the school yearbook.

205. If the job you're applying for doesn't require the Ph.D. that you just happen to have, leave that educational attainment off your resume. If the interviewer asks you specifically about having a Ph.D. during the interview, be honest. Just don't bring it up and risk losing the job because you're considered "overqualified." This fear runs deep among some employers, who automatically assume that you'll be out the door the minute you can get a job that makes use of your lofty degree.

206. Don't flunk the job-hunt test by exaggerating wildly, trying to pass yourself off as "God's gift to sports medicine administration." If you're new to the field, it's OK to say so, but it's not OK to come across as an overbearing egotist who will honor a company by taking a job there. In other words, don't ask to run the place, or say that you plan to manage it by the time you've been there one year. The current manager may take offense, and she probably has a say in whether or not you get hired.

207.

Don't overplay the "I-love-your-company" card. Sure, every company owner has a bit of vanity about having his own business; he has earned it through blood, sweat, tears, and fears. But if you make your resume one gigantic love-note tribute to the company ("a rose by any other name would not be Merit Corporation"), you won't be taken seriously.

208.

Don't write a sleazy resume. Sounding like you would go straight to the casting couch just to get your foot in the door will only get you a job as "the tramp next door." Play it straight and be ethical. Don't tell the interviewer on the phone or in your resume that you'll do "anything" to get an interview.

209.

Avoid playful language, or you may remind the hiring manager how very young (or immature) you are, which probably won't help your case.

210.

Make it clear why you're sending a resume by placing a skills summary at the start—or an objective directed at the field you want to enter.

211.

Check with your friends and contacts to see if you can locate a former or current employee who can tell you what the company values in its employees. However, don't just call up a total stranger who works there and try to pick his brain; that way, you run the risk of being dismissed totally (that person may pass on the message that "some freaky person applying for a job" tried to pry insider info out of him).

212.

Play up part-time jobs, experiences, and kudos that relate directly to the job you're trying to land. Don't just present the employer with your mishmash laundry list; he won't sort through it—instead, he'll toss it.

213.

Use the section heading "Experience," rather than "Employment History," if you don't have an employment history because you haven't held any jobs.

7.

Soccer Mom Resumes (Does Carpooling Count?)

All experience translates to the workplace. So, if you have spent the last twenty years raising children and being a homemaker, you definitely have plenty of skills, but you need to write a resume that will highlight these accomplishments well. While you may find resume-writing a bit of a challenge if you're a parent returning to the workforce, just take the time to do it right, and you will indeed walk away with exactly what you want—a paid position.

Here are some tips for people who have, in recent years, focused on children and the home front:

214. Be sure the resume-reader does not have to sort through vague terms meant to camouflage the fact that you were a stay-at-home mother. Just be up front and brassy about it; boast of what you've learned in the trenches and showcase those skills in an in-your-face kind of way.

215. Be realistic. You may need to target a first job that will help you gain skills. Set up your resume with that in mind, and try to zero in on that dream position later.

216. Prepare a resume that's easily customized. Remember, you may have to put the job you really want on the back burner until you rack up a few job credentials. It's OK to face that you may not immediately hop right into the position you truly want for a lifetime.

217.

Do several resumes because you should consider anything and everything. Don't be too quick to say, "I can't do that," or "I don't want to do that." If a job as a dog groomer is the only one you can get first time around, take it. You'll rack up some kudos for people pleasing, animal handling, and appointment scheduling, all of which can translate into other jobs.

218.

Understand where the focus of your resume should lie. If you've had nothing but teen jobs as a burger-flipper, you would be smart to highlight the skills you have gained in your years of running a household and taking care of children.

219.

Think of the things you're good at, and consider how those would translate in the job world. In other words, let's say you're a great organizer, which means you run your family like a drill sergeant. In the corporate community, this would translate to "strong organizational skills that are perfect for keeping an office running smoothly, a workforce humming along efficiently, a supervisor abreast of his or her schedule and obligations."

220. Don't forget to include the interpersonal skills you perfected while raising children, carpooling, and being a Girl Scout troop leader. This could translate to "excellent interpersonal skills that come from years of experience in dispute-resolution, schedule coordination, and preparedness training."

221. Be sure to list any part-time jobs and enumerate the skills/duties inherent in those.

222. Highlight your years of supervising a cook, nanny, housekeeper, and gardener because these translate to "experienced in diplomatic supervision of staff and adept at team problem-solving."

223. List that you have polished the skills required in taking care of a baby. In doing this, you present yourself as a candidate for a job as a nanny, day care worker, church worker, social worker's assistant, etc.

224. List that you have planned and managed the activities of toddlers and school-age kids. If you have been actively involved in the things your children do (clubs, sports, classes, church), you undoubtedly know kids—and this can translate into any number of jobs related to children: childcare facility worker or director, teacher's aide, cafeteria worker, church-nursery staffer, etc. Using skills closely akin to child-care jobs are ones at facilities for seniors, such as assisted-living apartments and such. You can apply to be recreation director, fitness leader, resident/facility liaison, or field-trip bus driver.

225.

List that you have developed time-efficiency expertise. Many busy business executives, doctors, and lawyers need staffers to help keep them on track and going in the right direction. A mere planner or Palm Pilot rarely does the job if a VIP has lots of irons in the fire. Show how you have turned multitasking into a fine art and kept family members on track for years and someone may be willing to give you a chance at a very interesting job.

226. List that you have done years of individualized cooking. Any restaurant kitchen needs some entry-level assistants who are willing to work their way up in the ranks. Knowing your way around a kitchen will help you land one of these jobs. This could segue into a job as a personal chef.

227. List that you have chauffeured (kids). Think how this one translates: limo driving, delivering flowers and other merchandise, and serving as an assistant to an elderly person.

228. List that you have accurately managed appointment scheduling. If you want a job as a receptionist, executive assistant, or secretary, the ability to manage a busy person's appointments is an important one.

229. List that you have shopped for a family. A person who has catered to the diverse needs of a family for years definitely knows how to shop.

230. Concentrate on other skills (like those above) that can be considered transferable. These assets could make you eligible for a number of interesting paid positions.

231. List any auxiliary work that you've done. Play up some of the "creative" aspects of parenting: arts-and-crafts instruction, scrapbooking, photography, party-planning. All of these are saleable skills, too.

232.

Do take temporary assignments in order to beef up the skills portion of your resume. Sign up with temp agencies and get started working.

233. Convey in your resume the fact that a hardworking person offers a good value for the money. You know all about hard work.

234. Play up your networking abilities. Most stay-at-home moms become quite adept at finding the right person for the right job, whether you're looking for a gardener, a volunteer worker, or a scriptwriter for the school play. On your resume, you can present yourself as an able-bodied and innovative networker who would make a good employee of a nonprofit organization, for example, which needs someone who has connections and knows how to use them. A public relations agency can also use someone like you.

235. Submit your resume very soon after you see a position advertised in the newspaper. And, in your cover letter, be sure to refer to the ad and the date it appeared.

236. Show openness to contract work. Because you have a dearth of concrete workplace experience, an employer may want to give you a "trial run" at first. The advantages for you are many: you will get to sample different business environments, computer systems, employee-rapport situations, and each time you do a job, you develop more skills that will help to beef up your resume and make you a more valuable asset to a company.

237. Use professional recruiters or headhunters to help you look for work. If your job search encompasses several different geographic areas, work with job experts in the particular regions. (See Chapter 27 for information on recruiters.)

238. Have a headhunter review your baseline resume before you finalize it. Ask for an honest critique of the wording, the skills listed, and the way you set up the resume. Then, take advantage of the advice and revise, revise, revise!

239. Don't get discouraged or offended when your resume merits little excitement from headhunters. These people are in business to place people in jobs. If they can find a job for you, they will. Naturally, they get more enthused over the job candidates who have excellent job histories and skills. Wouldn't you if you were in their shoes? But rest assured that they will get excited about your resume when you have had time to augment it with experience.

240.

Remember that a headhunter offers the advantage of focusing full-time on the job market and also becoming familiar with you and your background. Plus, if you get a job offer, a headhunter is usually a good negotiator and can sometimes get you more money for the job.

241.

Don't just sign up with a headhunter and then curl up to watch *Oprah* and take afternoon naps. Stay aggressive about your own job-hunting efforts. No one wants you to get a job as badly as you want it.

242.

Contact your network of personal and professional point people for job leads. Ask them if you can forward them copies of your resumes just in case. Tell family members, acquaintances, and all of your buddies that you're looking for a job. Ask them to give you any leads that seem appropriate for your background.

243. Check out dubious references. If you want to list someone who's familiar with your skills—a nonprofit where you did volunteer work, for example—but you're not sure that the supervisor gives good references, have a recruiter or a friend call to check out the reference. Suggest a few questions the caller could ask such as: How would you describe this employee's work habits? Was she dependable? How would you rate her communication skills? Was she able to get along well with others at the volunteer center?

244. Choose a supervisor or a fellow volunteer when you need a volunteer-job reference for your list of references.

245. Don't explain on your resume why you're looking for a job (divorce, poverty, kids now in school). Simply approach the job search just like any other job-hunter would. The fact that you've been a stay-at-home mom for twenty years doesn't have to enter into your resume apologetically. Be proud of what you've done!

246. If a hiring manager calls to quiz you further, don't lapse into apologies for not having more real jobs on your resume. Stick with what's important—that you have valid skills and a strong work ethic that will translate very well in the job market. The only thing you need is a chance to strut your stuff.

247. Resist the temptation to list your children's names and ages on your resume. That gives the impression that you will be an employee who talks about her kids constantly (instead of getting work done), and some employers don't like to hire people who shoulder the responsibility of several children. Also, overkill on the "personal" part of a resume is always a mistake. Keep your vision clear; the hiring manager isn't interviewing for a new best friend—he wants an excellent employee.

248. Include duties you've had while caring for an elderly parent. For example, if you serve as dear old dad's bookkeeper, portfolio manager, groundskeeper, household organizer, and estate executor, flaunt those skills on your resume.

249. Use restraint in handling questions about periods of unemployment or that job you held working for your spouse. Be careful what you say, and take the less-is-more approach. Your personal life is personal; just keep it that way. All too often, people make the mistake of "sharing" too much during interviews or in resumes, and the result is nothing positive. Usually, a hiring manager is wary of someone who gets too friendly too fast. Visions of you hanging around the water cooler and chatting all day long will come to mind.

250. Do not list "divorced" or "single parent" on your resume. Some people involved in a job search mistakenly think that such descriptions will gain them some sympathy and perhaps, in the process, a job. Not true. It's more likely that the hiring manager will be put off by your disclosure, or wonder if single parenthood really translates "encumbered with home duties and won't make a reliable employee." Make sure your resume doesn't refer to your separation, divorce, or marital status; you shouldn't feel compelled to divulge this information. Few interviewers go down that road, for fear of retribution (it's against the law to discriminate against you for your divorce, for having three kids that take up a lot of time, etc.).

251. If you're getting a divorce and hunting for a job, you and your children may be dealing with financial pressures, but it's important not to sound needy or desperate in your resume, on the phone, or during an interview. The hiring manager doesn't know you, and if you try to get a job by inviting him to your pity party, he probably will make a point of not knowing you. Companies steer clear of emotional basket cases—and wisely so. This means that even though you may feel close to tears every time you send out a resume or talk to someone on the phone about an interview, you must keep this part of you private.

252.

Be professional; sound upbeat; expect to talk to a hiring manager who is looking for a good employee, not a new best friend who will understand that you're going through a weepy period.

253. Be assertive in your follow-up. A week after you send a resume to a company, call to confirm that the human resources director received it. Take that opportunity to ask if that person has any questions.

8.

The Back-in-the-Saddle-Again Resume

You will probably want to set up your resume differently if you're returning to the workforce after a sabbatical, retirement, or unwanted joblessness. Let's say you're a gray-haired granddad, or you're newly divorced and desperate for work, or you are physically challenged and worry that someone will hold this against you, or that you were just released from federal prison and worry that you'll never get another job because of the stigma. Well, you're right in thinking that your special case requires special handling when it comes to resume writing, but there are plenty of ways to present yourself in a positive light that will get a hiring manager's attention—and, hopefully, snag you an interview.

Realistically, some companies do have biases against one or more of these circumstances, but that doesn't mean there aren't plenty of employers you can win over. Just imagine that you're the one doing the hiring—wouldn't you be willing to give an underdog a chance? That knowledge alone should motivate you. Stay pumped up by remembering how very much you've learned from your years of working and be prepared to put that asset in writing, in an excellent resume. You have skills; you're a seasoned veteran. These are good things that you can market. Just don't refer to yourself as "gramps" or "grandma" when turning in a resume to a hiring manager who is forming first impressions. You are only as vital as your present yourself. There are no points for being eccentric.

Those things said, you may want to follow the following tips for marketing yourself in a resume if you've been away from the working world for some time:

254. Put your education first on the resume only if you're in education and still looking for a job in that field. Otherwise, education should not be the first area listed on your resume.

255. Include a summary at the start of your resume because this helps the hiring manager get a sense of what you're all about and what you bring to the table. The summary can replace the objective, especially if including both would be repetitive. In your summary, explain why you qualify for the particular job opening. Having to wade through your massive experience and skills may be daunting enough to turn the hiring manager away so that he goes on to the next simple resume in the stack.

256. Write a resume that presents a well-qualified job candidate. Shy away from selling yourself as "an old codger" or "a gal who looks good for her age." If you think of yourself as over-the-hill, and project that image in your job hunt, it's not going to help you land interviews, much less a job.

257. If you've been away from the workforce for many years, you probably should choose the functional format (see chapter 4). This is a good way to illustrate what you can do for the employer and keep the emphasis away from your age and any negative connotations attached to it.

258.

If you're a gray-haired guy or gal, don't feel compelled to list all forty-five jobs you've held in a lifetime. In fact, even if you're dying to list them because you're proud of them, don't do it. Looking old isn't a plus in the competitive world of job search. If you're a veteran of the job-hunting wars, play up your skills and play down the fact that you've had a zillion jobs.

259.

Make yourself stand out from the crowd by doing lots of research on the company you want to become a part of, and customize your resume to fit the corporate culture of that company and to show that you're aware of its needs. You should find out all you can about the job opening; check out the company's website, and try to talk to a former employee of the company or a competitor who is familiar with the company, etc. In your search, if you discover a big negative (the company is shaky), just proceed as if you had never unearthed that information (the exception would be if that piece of information changes your mind about pursuing the job).

260. Weigh the impact of your experience and skills carefully in order to decide what to include in your resume. Your long career means you have to throw out some things, but it's also important to choose inclusions wisely.

261. Don't feature dates in the education portion of your resume, because those are a sure signal of your generation. A hiring manager will still know, of course, that you opted out because you heard that advertising your age wouldn't be politically correct, but it's still better than having all those years too obvious as the resume is passed around the office in a group of thirty-somethings.

262. Take advantage of applying for jobs online. See chapters 24 and 25 on e-resumes and resume scanning. If you don't know how to do this, get someone to help you.

263. If you're a senior who prides himself on being computer illiterate, make this your best-kept secret during job-search days. Don't brag about being out-of-sync with the 2004 workplace. Hiring managers won't share your amusement over being uniquely "low-tech." In fact, this is probably the surest way to get pegged as an old geezer who is too out of the loop to be employable.

If you want to switch careers (you want no part of the same old gig you did for thirty years), it's a good idea to get some Internet and computer skills under your belt first. You must be able to use word processing and spreadsheet programs, to email and do Internet research. (As one supervisor says, "I don't care what method they use to access information, but they need to be able to look up info on the Net...")

264. Show that you stay abreast of political correctness. Today, you use the word "teaming," not "teamwork." The workplace has "workers with disabilities," not "handicapped workers." We encourage "diversity," not "openness to all ethnicities." People can make judgments based on such things, so watch what you write on your resume.

If you plan to work with the public in the position you're seeking, don't say anything on your resume or cover letter about your comfort level in dealing with people of different races: "I don't have anything against blacks or Mexicans," for example, wouldn't be a statement that would advance you toward the hiring finals. Hiring managers today will assume that you have no prejudices; to point out that you don't only raises eyebrows and suspicion concerning your real stand on this issue.

265. Dilute titles that sound dated or pompous. Today's job titles are more down-to-earth, so if you think one of your old job titles will make you seem like a relic of worlds past, simply knock down the language a few pegs, to something less ostentatious.

266.
Underscore your ability to solve and finesse problems calmly and effectively. Veterans have an edge in this respect; you've seen more, experienced more, and fewer things send you into fits and hysterics.

267. Express your willingness to carry a heavy load. Sometimes, oldsters have a distinct advantage in having worn many hats in jobs they held when times were tough economically in the U.S., so this is a good point to emphasize in your favor.

268. Describe your comfort level with coworkers and supervisors. You can base this assertion on the fact that you have had varied job experiences that taught you a great deal about working toward the greater good of the company.

269. Illustrate that you're a good multi-tasker. This is one prejudice that some hiring managers and supervisors admit to having when it comes to hiring (or not hiring) older people. "I'm afraid this salesman will be good at sales, but woefully inept at keeping his records because our office is completely networked." Let your resume show that you can do whatever the job requires; if you aren't proficient at a certain vital program, start learning it right now—or express your confidence that you're a quick study.

270. Don't try to bluff your way into a job. If the company contact mentions something on the phone that you're not familiar with, don't pretend to know what he's talking about. It's OK to ask: "Exactly what do you mean by *consensus building*?"

271. Emphasize the contributions you can make to the company by touting those you've made to companies in the past. Stay on message. Keep the self-talk positive: You are an expert in the field who has many years of experience, and that's competence taken to an all-new level. Don't feel self-conscious just because you're older.

272. Keep the information in your resume relevant to the position you're trying to get. Don't fly off on tangents—a common pitfall. Rambling talkers often aren't very productive, and most workplaces already have enough.

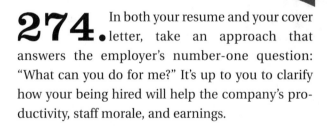

273.

Take advantage of networking opportunities. Join an executives' breakfast club. Let people at your church know that you're job hunting. Put out the word in all of your club and exercise facilities. Using your list of contacts may be the way a new job comes to your attention.

274. In both your resume and your cover letter, take an approach that answers the employer's number-one question: "What can you do for me?" It's up to you to clarify how your being hired will help the company's productivity, staff morale, and earnings.

275. Under the heading Work Experience, you can include items such as volunteer work, charity chairperson gigs, and freelance assignments. However, don't include this kind of experience if it was something you did more than a decade ago.

276. To show that you can scale down your expectations (you spent twenty years as a store manager, but you now simply want a job in retail—not the one at the helm), explain this preference when you go in for an interview, but don't go into too much explanation on your resume. It may come across in a bad way: "I got sick of people when I was a manager." Or: "I'm tired of working hard so I'd like to cruise for a few years." Instead, mention the things you can do well, and tell the hiring manager how these skills will transfer to a position in retail sales or stocking shelves or whatever the job listing is.

277. Make sure your resume has enough fleshing out in the job skills department to show why you qualify for the job that was listed even though your last job was totally unrelated. Don't leave it up to the hiring manager to translate your skills to the current job; instead, you do the work of explaining why you're a good fit for real-estate officer secretary when your last job was first-grade teacher. Be convincing and you'll probably land an interview.

278. Lead with information that can illustrate how well you qualify for the position that is open. If you're a former high school principal who now wants a job in department-store customer service, your skill list should feature pertinent items: "conflict resolution, good communication skills, and strong rapport with clients." Think it through, and you can find ways that any recent past experience will be of value in the new job slot.

279. Address the question "What will you do if a problem arises that you don't know the answer to?" This is something that may be on the mind of the hiring manager when he's considering someone who has been out of the workforce for a number of years. Do you know how to improvise? Are you a good self-starter? Are you quick to problem-solve? Do you take the initiative to find answers to problems or are you going to try to talk to everyone in nearby cubicles before you make your move?

280. Emphasize your ability to focus on a task and take a professional approach. Unless you're trying to get hired as a greeter at Kmart or Wal-Mart, you want the employer to know that you won't get lost in too much chitchat. Sometimes older people are perceived as overly "conversational" simply because they have been out of the workplace for a while. It's your job to create the image of yourself as a professional. Make your resume reflect that you're a hard-working, capable individual who can get the job done, doesn't waste coworkers' time, and is pleasant to work alongside.

281.

When you list any temp work you've done, there's no need to mention the temp firm itself; instead, list the companies you actually did work for. Again, list any achievements for which you were cited, or things you believe that you achieved on these jobs.

282. Remember that one sign of an ancient resume is that laundry list of "Personal" items. In another decade, it was fine to let employers know that you were a pickup basketball standout, or a dog-show ace, but in today's job world, this information is better left for the interview—and even then, you should only mention your hobbies, pastimes, and sports if you're asked about them.

283. Don't wave a flag that says "I couldn't be more low-tech." Don't send in a resume from a dot-matrix printer or typewriter unless you want to scream the message that you're out-of-step with today's technology. You want to send in a resume that has been written on a computer and printed on a laser printer.

If you don't own a computer, you probably know someone who does (your offspring, niece, nephew, grandchild). If not, you can go to a community center, a library, or hire someone to do your resume preparation.

284. Try to find someone who's willing to swear by your talents. When you're actively searching for a job, a company will be more likely to give you a chance if someone vouches for you, listing your strong points. When someone provides a testimonial to your abilities and workplace viability and prowess, it goes a long way toward getting you an interview. If this person is a former coworker or supervisor, be sure to list him or her on your reference list and draw attention to the endorsement in your cover letter. This can put you out in front of other contenders.

285.

When you call to verify that your resume arrived, sound energetic and be sure the exchange is brief and to the point. Sometimes, seniors can hook a hiring manager with a good resume and then ruin their chances by keeping the person on the phone too long. For the hiring manager, this is an ominous precursor of chattiness that would undoubtedly be a part of your employee package. This won't get you any points considering the fact that traditionally most job settings have trouble with wasted time due to socializing. Why advertise the fact that you're a major-league talker? Keep in mind that most companies want to increase productivity, not stall it.

286. It is better to put the emphasis on what you can do well, thanks to all those years of working—not how old you are. Our society does have age bias, whether we like it or not, and you will find that in the workplace just like everywhere else. Work with it, not against it, to become gainfully employed once again.

287. Don't "feature" your incarceration on your resume. Do, however, be honest during your interview. You must reveal that you have a criminal record; if you're dishonest about this and are found out, you could be fired. If you want to work at a department store and you have a record for shoplifting, the employer has a right to decide whether she wants to give you a chance. He may choose to be optimistic and hire you.

288. If you're physically challenged, reveal this information on a resume only if the physical challenge will affect your ability to do this job. For example, if you want to be a recreation director at a senior-living facility and you are wheelchair-bound, you should say so on your resume, but also offer reassurance that you know how to work around this and it will not keep you from doing a good job.

289. If you're a recovering drug/alcohol abuser, you must reveal this information if it will affect your ability to do the job—or if it pertains to the setting where you want to work. An example would be an AA member who wants to be a bartender. You must be up front, and let the prospective employer make the call. You may be certain that you can handle a partying atmosphere; he may or may not agree.

9.

Know What's Expected in an Artsy Field

Some off-the-wall resumes don't follow the traditional route of resume writing. An example is a resume that you prepare for a profession that is known for being unconventional. Use an unorthodox resume only if you are sure that it is acceptable in the field you want to enter. It's important to remember that the difficulty with seeking a job in some of the "unique" industries is that the wrong look or feel to a resume can land it in the trash quicker than in any other field. Snobbery abounds, and these hiring managers know what they like and that's that.

Some tips for special-field resumes include:

290. Make sure that you also include all of the required elements of a regular resume (see chapters 1 and 2).

291. You're allowed a bit of leeway if you're in an artistic profession, but generally speaking, keep your resume simple and make your portfolio samples the parts that sparkle and sell your skills. A resume that's hard to read because it's done in fancy script or has a "designy" format may distract the reader rather than draw him in for closer scrutiny.

292. If you're involved in theater, you still must open with a summary statement that sells, just like you would if you were a lawyer, teacher, or doctor. You can't get away with a simple laundry list of your movie/stage credits; that won't do the sales job for you. Your resume may go up against some candidates who are more creative in their resume approaches, and the resumes that sell are the ones that net auditions.

293.

If you're looking for a job in an artistic field, you can make your resume dazzle and sparkle. But don't go overboard, trying to sound like a wild-and-crazy "creative" who will do anything, no matter how off-the-wall. Instead, highlight yourself as a professional: "Experienced photo stylist interested in gaining magazine-staff experience and flexible about contract work versus full time."

294.

Mention in your cover letter the availability of your portfolio of work samples. Don't attach this to your resume, or insist that the hiring manager look at it. Naturally, you want to showcase your talent if you're an artist, fashion designer, architect, graphic artist, advertising or PR wizard, photographer, photo stylist, or any other professional whose work can best be seen by pictures, not words. But having someone take the time to look at your portfolio usually won't happen unless you win an interview. Use a three-ring binder and include a table of contents to show what's inside; typical components are work samples (your best stuff), resume, testimonials, award certificates, media clips, licenses.

295. If you're a hairstylist or in another art field that has a regular and loyal clientele, it's a good idea to include customer testimonials in your reference list, not your resume. This is helpful because otherwise, a prospective employer has nothing to go on except your word ("I have a loyal following of four thousand who will be coming to have me do their hair at the new salon, too!").

296.
Understand that in the design field, the choice of font or a bad design may get your resume in the trash much more quickly than lack of experience.

297. Don't be pitiful in your resume or cover letter. Example: "Having looked everywhere in town and having been rejected by everyone, I hope that you will give me a chance."

298. Don't say that you're "willing to do anything" to get on board, which comes across as desperate.

299. In artistic fields, don't try to sound like an old pro when the hiring manager can take a quick glance at your resume and see that you're fibbing.

300. Don't name-drop to try to make the hiring person believe you're a "real actor."

301. Don't pad your artistic resume with mentions of workshops, etc. that you know will impress unless you actually attended (knowing someone who went there doesn't count).

302. Don't overdo it. Interviewers in the arts fields recognize fakery faster than anyone, and they truly look down on fraud more than they do a record of zero experience.

303. Emphasize examples of your efforts at continuing education, which are always important in arts fields. If you've been an interior designer for twenty years, show proof that you have stayed aware of the changing trends and that you make a point of keeping relevant.

304. Be sure to include any awards you have won for projects or presentations. Explain what they mean; don't assume that an employer will understand how impressive it is that you were named "Top Producer" five years consecutively in dog-show pageantry production.

305. Designate any specific certifications you have received, such as FTD Master Designer (for florists). You don't need to amplify the well-known ones, but do give a run-down of those that are little-known—what it means that you were recognized by Pretty Posy Planners of America.

306. If you're in the fashion industry or graphic design, your portfolio is your main sales tool, and you should make sure that your resume or cover letter refers to its availability. Use your portfolio to set you apart; include projects you're most proud of and ones that show your talent and skills. You can work your way into the creative corridor by showing an excellent portfolio and a strong resume. Take into consideration the company you are targeting when you choose items to display in your portfolio; include the things that fit that company's particular "look," and don't include those items that would turn them off, or that aren't their style. You want to show the company what you have to offer insofar as taking their look to even higher levels of excellence. (Pick through your portfolios—the one you assembled for getting into design school, one for graduation, and one you compiled to enter the job market. Don't hesitate to include press clippings from trade publications and fashion magazines, and be sure to include work that brought you kudos.)

307. In describing your professional experience, be as specific as possible to give a clear picture of what your responsibilities were at each job you held. Don't assume that the interviewer will know; different firms delegate responsibilities to different positions, so your job title may not translate. For example, some magazines have managing editors edit copy, while others make this role strictly managerial, keeping the flow of each issue on schedule. If you've been a managing editor and you're trying to get a job as an editor-in-chief, you must prove that you've paid your dues editing other writers. You may want to mention in your cover letter that you have many samples of issues for which you did most of the copy editing.

308.

Emphasize elements of past jobs that are applicable to the one you are seeking.

309. Give the prospective employer a clear picture of your version of what this job is—in other words, if you are a wedding planner, what does your version of wedding planning mean? Be specific in the cover letter and resume.

310. If your field is makeup and hair design for a funeral home, explain how you approach doing these tasks for the deceased: Do you consult with the family to get their preferences, do you improvise, or do you have a one-size-fits-all approach?

311. If you're a novice at the profession and you're trying to get your foot in the door, you can list creative awards won in school—high school and college—and explain what these mean. But if you're a veteran of twenty or more years, a stroll down that historical avenue will make it seem like you're desperate. A forty-year-old who is still bragging about winning the county fair poster contest in seventh grade is going to make a hiring manager look askance at the resume.

312. If you have spent periods freelancing, give a very clear delineation of your activities. Did you work with a number of commercial clients? Did you seek work actively or rely on referrals? How busy were you? Did you stay so busy you had to turn down work?

313. Include any ongoing independent study that you're doing. Give details on the type of course, why it's relevant, how it will beef up your bag of tricks.

314. Toot your own horn when it comes to your skills because creative types must do so in order to get hired: "Showed strong design skills, won praise of editorial staffers for the designs for their features, etc."

315.

Even though your field may be esoteric, you can still seize opportunities to spotlight ways in which your work affected the bottom line; for example, you can show that your work as a showroom display designer increased sales by 15 percent within two months of your hire date. Specify, specify! Don't hesitate to pat yourself on the back for work that won praise; that's the part of your resume that a hiring manager will focus on the most.

316.
Give plenty of details about the scope of your job; in other words, if you're a personal chef, you can indicate if this meant catering huge dinner parties for high-profile guests—or if you made three meals a day for a person who was confined to bed because of illness.

317.
In fields such as graphic art, be sure to specify if you created designs or brought to fruition the designs someone else created.

318. If you want to look like a shoo-in for a directorship (fashion, art, print, theater, design), you must emphasize leadership and team-building skills. Often, the interviewer will be looking for signs of the prima donna in the arts fields, so it's up to you to set yourself apart from the divas by pinpointing how well you get along with subordinates, peers, and management. On the other hand, if you haven't related well with coworkers in the past, keep it to yourself; you can't sell yourself in a way that isn't based on the truth, but you also don't have to flaunt that you're the Bad Seed, either.

319. Emphasize your ingenuity and creativity. If you're in any of the arts fields, from personal cooking or shopping to wedding planning to landscape design, it's important to underscore your ability to come up with striking new ideas.

320. Don't highlight knowledge or skills that may be considered irrelevant. That's the mark of a novice resume writer—and, by the same token, a novice "creative." The fact that you painted scenery for your high-school musical won't be of much interest to a big-league Broadway director. On the other hand, if you served as an assistant to an author, and you're seeking an entry-level job with a publishing company, this former job will interest the employer.

321. Highlight the skills that will make the prospective employer visualize you in a key role (not as a flunky). Just because you have swept up for the photo studio's head photographer or made babies laugh with squeaky stuffed animals doesn't mean you have to point out the way you "paid your dues" in the business.

322. Don't be surprised if, in addition to your resume, you are asked to submit work samples that are "raw" and "unedited." It is hard for hiring managers to determine what kind of graphic artist or writer you are if you've only had jobs in which a higher-up (art director or editor) cleaned up your work, making the final product more polished than the original. Thus, they will want to see what you can do on your own. If your work takes lots of editing or bringing up to par, that makes you a less desirable candidate than someone whose work is closer to what the supervisor wants.

323.

Somewhere in your resume, emphasize that you can meet deadlines (if this is one of your strong points). In the worlds of "creatives," being unstructured and sometimes tardy is often a problem. Making yourself stand out as both talented and punctual will truly set you apart from the crowd.

324. Don't emphasize your bent for steamrolling. Lots of people in artistic fields like to run the show, but that's not always a plus that you should feature on a resume. For example, you may believe strongly that being a domineering wedding planner works; you steer the mother of the bride away from the bride's dressing room, make sure that the ringer bearer and flower girl are stopped at the end of the aisle by designated handlers, and supervise things in a fairly heavy-handed way. But some clients may regard this as a Soup-Nazi approach to running a wedding. Instead, stress the way you "listen" to what your clients want and try to deliver within those boundaries.

10.

Write an Effective Resume for Flexible Work Styles

Employees today are asking for flexible work styles, and some employers are receptive to the idea because they want to keep talented employees. The option of having a flexible work style may become a reality via skillful communication, employee to employer.

By definition, job sharing means two or more people sharing a single job. For people who want to achieve balance between work and personal needs, this is a popular choice. To present this approach as a viable concept, you need to know how to create a resume that pitches the idea of job sharing and other alternate forms of employment, such as telecommuting and flextime. (Telecommuting is using telecommunication—computer, phone, modem—to work outside the traditional office or workplace, usually at home or in a mobile situation. Telecommuters can log on and access their company's network just as if they were actually in the office. Flextime is putting in the same number of hours other employees do but on a different schedule—for example, working 7 to 4 instead of 8 to 5.)

Here are some ideas for resumes for flexible work styles:

325. Find your partner before you prepare the job-share resume and job-share proposal. In most cases, if you're proposing a job-share arrangement, you will want to identify your job-share partner before writing a resume and job-share proposal.

326. Be careful when choosing a job-share partner. Finding a compatible partner is the most important aspect of this plan. Your fellow job sharer must have a background similar to yours and a resume that boasts skills much like yours. Otherwise, it will be impossible to "fill in" for each other when the need arises.

327.
Search for an in-company job-share partner if you are currently employed.

328. If you are approaching a new employer, enlist his ideas in finding a compatible and interested job-share partner.

329. Review coworkers as prospects for job-sharing partners. If you pair up with another valued worker, your supervisor may be even more eager to accommodate you and manage to retain both you and the other employee.

330. Check out your business network. Professional groups, chambers of commerce, and trade groups are good places to look for a job-share partner. Find out if there are other people who share your work outlook and goals.

331. Peruse your personal network (friends and family)—often a promising resource for a job-share partner.

332. Tap university and community college placement offices for possible job-share partners, such as grad students, and when you find someone, explain the setup on your job-sharing resume.

333. Check with employment agencies. Agencies may be a long shot if you want a flexible job style because companies usually hire recruiters to fill traditional job openings. However, it is becoming more common for employment agencies to provide employees to work hourly, part-time, and flextime. Check to see if a recruiter can suggest a job-share partner or a flexible position for you.

334. Advertise for a job-share buddy. If you search through your regular networking sources and fail to come up with a partner, try placing an ad in the newsletter of your professional group or a neighborhood newspaper. Describe your novel approach to the working world and see if you get any takers.

335.

The resume must show your current employer why switching you to a job-share situation will help him and not result in extra work or too much extra expense. Typically, the employees who are allowed special working arrangements are top performers who bring so much to the worktable that the employer wants to be accommodating.

336.

Propose the idea of a job-sharing setup in your resume. Two professionals want an arrangement that allows them to remain at the functional level they had, via job sharing. On the other hand, hourly workers can simply cut back on their hours to enhance their work/life balance.

337.

Do a job-sharing resume if you think this plan would work well for you because you're raising children, you want to pursue higher education, you're approaching retirement, or you simply want a more balanced existence.

338. Don't assume you have a legal right to do job sharing. There is no legal right to flexible work arrangements of any kind. The Civil Rights Act of 1964 prohibits discrimination against certain protected classes—gender, race, creed, and age (40 or older). Later legislation covers those individuals with disabilities. But nowhere in the employment laws, including wage and hour laws, is there legislation that mandates flexible work styles.

339. Assume the responsibility for proving your case. If you want an alternate work style, it's your job to prove how this can benefit an employer. A large company (200+ employees) or one that's publicly held will probably reap some very good media coverage for accommodating employees who want flexible work styles.

340. Your job-share resume looks much like a typical resume, but should be tailored to highlight the benefits of work flexibility. Use a well-designed reverse chronological or functional resume.

341. If you want to share a job with someone, mesh your resume with that of your job-share partner. Usually, you find your own job-share partner and then go to an employer with that person and a plan for the job-sharing arrangement.

342. List duties and responsibilities that you and the coworker will perform. Also list your duties and responsibilities at your current employer and previous employers in the past three to five years. Make these duties and responsibilities, coupled with those of your job-share partner, the cornerstone of your job-share search.

343. Spotlight accomplishments. Whether you're applying for a job share within your existing company or with a new company, showcasing your accomplishments is vital. Accomplishments are the difference between just warming a chair and adding value. The employer may know you worked there, but what did you do that made a difference for your department, division, or company? Prove that you're a value-added and a company is more likely to agree to what you want.

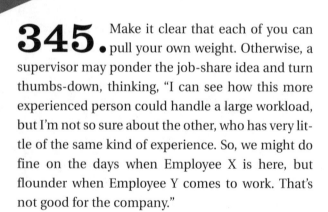

344.

Explain how the coordinated effort will work. Join with your job-share partner to make sure your resumes fit together; both resumes must show logical similarities in duties, responsibilities, and accomplishments. You must have overlapping skills and experience or it won't make sense for you to share the same job.

345.

Make it clear that each of you can pull your own weight. Otherwise, a supervisor may ponder the job-share idea and turn thumbs-down, thinking, "I can see how this more experienced person could handle a large workload, but I'm not so sure about the other, who has very little of the same kind of experience. So, we might do fine on the days when Employee X is here, but flounder when Employee Y comes to work. That's not good for the company."

346. Show flexibility. When you ask for a special work arrangement such as job sharing, flextime, or telecommuting, you're usually getting preferential treatment over other employees, so if you expect favors, you need to be flexible. If your supervisor occasionally asks you to work four or eight hours longer due to seasonal work or some business crisis, be prepared to cooperate.

347. Underscore the seamlessness of your partnership. A good way to increase your chances of getting a job share is to show how your background and that of and your job-share partner add up to more than enough to get the job done. Start with the job description and write both resumes to cover all required and preferred areas of the job description. Don't list skills that you and your job-share partner don't have, but use the job description as a guide to write the resume.

348. Prepare a proposal for job-sharing. If you're an existing employee or are applying for a job-share position with a new company, write a job-share proposal. This document illustrates how and why this arrangement will benefit both you and the organization.

349. File a request for a rearrangement. The request outlines exactly what type of arrangement you want with your job share—hours, days, times, responsibilities. You can write a proposal that does or does not include a job-share partner, but it's better to include a job-share partner to simplify the thought process for company officials. This also shows the thoroughness and seriousness you're dedicating to this undertaking.

350.

Make it clear how the work will get done. Offer an analysis of how the responsibilities of the job will be accomplished.

351. Include a schedule for each job-share partner—which days and hours each of you will work.

352. Discuss how you will communicate with each other during the week to make sure that the work is completed.

353. Outline ways in which you will document your work and the status of the work on a daily basis so that your employer can see how continuity of services will be provided for external and internal clients.

354. Make it easy for the company to understand how two will do the work of one.

355. Clarify how job-sharing benefits the company. Job-sharing partners typically receive half their salary and often receive benefits as well. So, what guarantee does the company have that two of you will do the work as well as one good employee? How will the company see a benefit from the sharing of a job?

356. Point out that someone will always be available; if one employee has to call in sick, the other can come to the rescue. That way, projects never suffer.

357. Underscore that the employer gets two employees for the price of one. One of the biggest benefits for the company is the payoff of what two experienced employees bring to the table. A duo can attack every aspect of doing the job.

358. Include in your job-sharing resume/proposal a budget that lists the cost of both salaries and the cost of both sets of benefits the job-sharers get. Show the cost of salaries and benefits, the cost of one employee, and the incremental difference. Make the proposal easy for them to use.

359. In your proposal, be sure to talk about the supervisory aspect—explain who will be in charge of reviews, employee discipline, etc. Spell out everything. Make the delineation of duties very clear; clarify who will do what and when. Make it easy for the company to see that you two can easily handle the responsibilities of the position without anything falling through the cracks.

360.

Spell out contingency plans. Show who will step in if one or both job-sharing partners are ill, there's a death in a family, or one partner must miss work to deal with a personal issue. Let the employer know that you plan to cover for each other and work the extra hours. This is a strong benefit because it will reduce absenteeism for the position.

361.

If you are applying for a job-share position with a new employer, make your resume and job-sharing proposal drive home the ways this plan will work to the advantage of the company. Corporations (and supervisors) tend to resist new approaches, so it's up to you to make the idea look like a win-win.

362.

Show that you're planning for the usual "hand-over" period of three to four weeks, during which time you will transition from a forty-hour-a-week style to a twenty-hour workweek.

363. Show that you understand how holidays affect job sharing. For regular employees to get holiday pay, many companies require working the day before and often the day after a holiday, and for job sharers, this can be an issue. That's why you need to spell out how you think holidays should be handled while you're still in the planning/proposal stage. A fair arrangement is for an employer to allow each job sharer half of each holiday.

364. Delineate how your supervisory job-sharing will work. When job-sharers are supervisors or managers, the staff may be required to report to the job-sharer on duty. Each may have certain responsibilities for staffers A, B, and C, or for specific areas of work. Coordination and liaison between job sharers is extremely important. However, a consistent and well-planned coordination between job sharers should go smoothly and not create any snags. If questions arise about who is responsible for what duty, you haven't done enough planning.

365. In your resume, propose sample schedules. Below is a sample:

Job Sharer 1: normally works Monday, Tuesday, Wednesday A.M.

Job Sharer 2: normally works Wednesday P.M., Thursday, Friday.

366. Illustrate how job-sharing fits your industry and position. Some of the industries that use job-sharing are: banking, financial services, primary and secondary education, universities, and public accounting.

367. Write a resume that sets you up for the nontraditional work style called telecommuting. Telecommuting is an alternate work arrangement that allows you to work from home and commute with the office via telephone, email, and fax. Much of communication within a corporation is done in that manner anyway, so this can be a reasonable method of working. Again, you must convince your supervisor that this saves time and money. Your not needing a desk or office, for example, automatically benefits the company.

368. Use your resume to propose flextime. Another common alternative work arrangement, flextime lets you work nontraditional work hours as long as you still finish your work. For example, instead of 8 AM to 5 PM, you may choose to work 10 AM to 7 PM, or 6 AM to 3 PM. Usually, you must be at work during the company's core hours—for example, 10 AM to 3 PM. Other than that, you are allowed flexibility in start and finish times.

11.

Customize Your Resume to Suit the Job

One of the best ways to hit a bull's-eye in the corporate world is by customizing every resume you send out. Instead of going the generic route, spend some time updating and fine-tuning your resume to suit the job description in the advertisement or listing. This shows your attention to detail and drives home the point that you really care about being considered for this job. Showing your interest and highlighting your skills are two keys to getting the job you want.

369. Write multiple resumes to facilitate job-hunting, and if necessary, customize in different ways. A variety of skills may come from various industries and job functions. If you're applying for a job similar to the one you had previously, and you have good job tenure, use reverse chronological format. If you're applying for a job that is different from your previous job, and your applicable experience is more than three to five years old or your job tenure is short, use a functional resume. With these two types of resumes, it will be relatively easy for you to customize your resume to the job.

370. Make your resume reflect your homework on the company. In the old days, if you wanted to find out information about a company, you had to go to the library and look up business information companies, Standard & Poor's or Moody's binders, or you could call the company and request an annual report and a 10K. But that's ancient history. Today, finding out information about a company is as easy as a few keystrokes. To investigate, check out its website; if you don't know where the website is, use a search engine to locate information on the company. Try MSN, Yahoo, Google, Alta Vista, or Ask Jeeves. You can use Hoovers.com to research publicly held companies and their subsidiaries. See Moody's at www.moodys.com and Standard & Poor's, www.standardandpoors.com.

371.

If you have several career goals, come up with separate resumes that reflect these goals—one for each. That way you can include a different objective with each one that is very specific and which will be more appealing to the person reading the resume.

372.
Pay attention to special industry considerations. If you are in the high-tech industry, your resume will highlight your computer skills and projects. If you are in a specialized field such as entertainment, your resume will also highlight projects versus continuity of work. If you're in a service industry (nannies, valet parkers, housekeepers), focus on the quality of experience you have gained from various employers. Anyone applying in industries such as high-tech, entertainment, or services may want to consider a functional or combination resume to present skills.

373.
Tweak your resume carefully when a job listing asks for a degree and you don't have one. Don't hesitate to apply for a job if you have the experience but not the degree. Highlight your applicable experience, and show the hiring manager how your experience will compensate for a lack of degree.

374. Customize by putting your Most Important Things first. The skills and experience that appear first in your list for each employer or first in a functional resume will be interpreted as Most Important. That means that you should rearrange your skills for each resume you do. Put the skills listed as requirements in the job posting first in your resume.

375. Supersize your experience if you're customizing your resume to apply for a job that requires more than you have. Underscore experience that relates to the job you are interviewing for. Emphasize accomplishments that show you're qualified and you've excelled and added value in that area.

376.
Customize your resume carefully if you're trying to soften your career changes. If you've switched job areas, which most people do at least three times in their working lives, couch this in positive terms by showing a logical thread to your career change. Most career changes are stepping stones. Don't write: "Hated engineering so much that I went back to law school." Instead, write: "Completed law degree after five successful years of engineering experience. Focused on patent law because of technical experience and legal expertise."

377. For a career change, write a functional resume. A great reason to customize your resume is for a career change. Changing careers is much more difficult than just changing jobs. So if you are trying to jump ship and go into a new endeavor, you will want to customize your resume to fit the job listing and use a functional resume to list applicable skills. Changing careers means that you are changing the type of position you're seeking, and this may mean changing industries, too.

378. Customize your downshifting resume to show how that will benefit a potential employer. Make your words upbeat—never woe-is-me. In a resume for downshifting, you must show this as a conscious choice (not a default choice). More and more people are choosing quality of life over compensation. Just explain in your cover letter that you bring outstanding experience to the job and that you want to trade that wealth of experience for the flexibility inherent in the job. Show that you're interested in the position and that you look forward to having a job with reduced workload and responsibility because you want the greatest of perks—more time.

379.

Customize your resume for a move. If you want to relocate, use a local address and telephone number to make it easier for the company to contact you. This is especially true if your field typically doesn't compensate workers for relocation. In that case, it's best to sound like a local candidate—even if you haven't actually made the move yet. Hiring someone new costs a company time and money, and hiring someone from out of town is even more difficult. Make it as easy as possible for the hiring manager to offer you the job.

380.

Also, be ready with a good reason for moving. Perhaps your grown daughter, her husband, and their child are relocating to L.A. and you want to be nearby—that's a good reason. But hiring managers may look askance at someone who is moving because he wants to surf or likes mountains. That can sound like a sign of "impulsivity disorder," which may make the company decide not to interview you. Other good reasons for a move: your spouse has been transferred, your elderly parents need you nearby, the industry you're in is flourishing in Wisconsin. Examples of moving to join your industry or make the most of your functional skills would be relocating to New York for its financial institutions, or to Silicon Valley (California) or Silicon Hills (Austin, Texas) for computer programming.

381. As you customize, weigh the advantages of functional versus chronological. The standard recommendation for resumes is to use a reverse chronological resume to showcase experience maximally and make it easy to see. But sometimes it makes sense to use a different format. If you have pertinent experience in a functional industry or managerial area that's more than three to five years old, consider building a functional resume that highlights the experience without placing a date on it. This allows you to capitalize on good experience without dating it by assigning it to a prior employer.

382. Accent with industry buzzwords as you customize. Every industry has its own special words, and using some illustrates your "in" status. Similarly, every position has relevant words, which you can include when applying for a certain job. (See chapters 24 and 25.)

383. Customize your resume for the computer. Now that resumes are scanned, or cut-and-pasted into the computer, you need to create copies of your resume in different versions. Write your resume and save it in both Plain Text and Rich Text. These options are available in Microsoft Word. Click: FILE, SAVE AS. Pull down the SAVE AS TEXT box and choose a text version. (See more in chapters 24 and 25.)

384. Your resume is a marketing tool, and you can often omit experience that isn't relevant to the job. But when you fill out a job application, include your entire work history. Applications typically include a sentence that you must sign testifying that you have included your entire background, so do exactly that.

385. Customize your resume to spotlight functional skills. Use a functional or reverse chronological resume to show positions that you have held that gave you specific kinds of experience. For example, if you have experience in real estate sales and real estate operations, write your resume to feature those two functional skills and accomplishments for each position.

386. Customize your resume for industry experience. Use a functional or reverse chronological resume to show the various industry sectors that you have worked in or where you have specific experience. For example, if you have experience in real estate and in the mortgage banking industries, write your resume to list those two industry skills and the various accomplishments in each industry.

387. Prepare a mix-and-match resume. Consider having the various elements of your resume as pieces (possibly even numbered) that you can mix and match in your resume to build a customized resume for each position you seek. This will allow you to have two main resumes: reverse chronological and functional. And you can come up with custom resumes for various jobs without creating two hundred different versions of your resume. This approach also streamlines the process and decreases confusion. When you send your resume and follow up, you need to know what version you sent, and that's easier to get mixed up than you may imagine.

388.

Customize your resume to show how well your skills match the requirements of the job. This makes it easy for the hiring manager to recognize the fact that you do have the desired skills. Look at the job description or ad and make sure that your resume lists those skills toward the top, because the first items the hiring manager reads are the ones he will view as most important.

389.

Leave off your education if it's going to hurt you in the race for a certain job.

If you have a Ph.D. in art history and you're applying for a job as an executive trainee in an oil-and-gas company, consider omitting that Ph.D. You may look overqualified for the job; plus, it's not going to help you get a job in that industry and in that functional area.

390.

Write your resume appropriately if you're overqualified in experience as well. For example, if you were an attorney for ten years and then went back to school to get your nursing degree, leave off the legal background if it doesn't apply to your medical experience.

391. When you customize, don't make yourself sound like a crusty old war veteran. If you are an older candidate, you may be viewed as too seasoned. Age bias isn't politically correct, but that doesn't stop a hiring manager from being skeptical of a resume with numerous years of experience. What's the answer? Edit your resume down to include only those years of experience that pertain to the job. That's not considered cheating, and it may improve your chances of getting an interview. (See more tips in chapter 8, the Back-in-the-Saddle-Again Resume.)

392. Customize your job titles to make them descriptive, not confusing. Is there a synonym for a job title that will make the duties and functions you performed clearer? If so, you may want to revise the name of the position and toss out the obtuse title that the company gave you when you worked there. For example, if you were hired as "receptionist," but you actually expanded the position and became your supervisor's liaison to the world outside the office, it may be more impressive to list yourself as Corporate Liaison on your resume. Or, if your title was Assistant III, that won't mean much to a hiring manager studying your resume. Try something more informative, like Senior Assistant to the Vice-President of Marketing. If necessary, explain to your interviewer that you revised your title for that job in a way that would be more recognizable in the business world.

Hint: Don't get too aggressive in your upward mobility. You can't call yourself CEO if you were the computer associate. You weren't a hair salon entrepreneur if you were the one who scheduled appointments.

393.

Make your resume effective by customizing the description of each company for which you worked. Emphasize items that affect that industry. For example, if you worked at a bank and you're once again applying to work for a bank, include details about the bank where you worked. You can say, for example, that the bank had $1.5 billion in assets, catered to a middle-market clientele in a regional area of your state, was a state or federally chartered bank, and give other details of interest in the banking industry. This kind of insider info makes it clear that you know whereof you speak.

394. Customize your extracurricular activities. Keep your professional and community activities as generic as possible. Typically, you should list professional and community activities that don't reference politics, religion, race, or gender. But if you're applying for a job where such a reference would be an advantage, absolutely include it.

395. Customize with explanations. If you've had frequent job changes, you may want to list your reasons for change at the end of each position. This lets the reader know why you have changed jobs so often. Supplying reasonable explanations for the changes may help you tear down any resistance you would get from a hiring manager who is on the alert for job-hopping candidates. This is a tactic that you may not want to use on every resume you send, but with some companies, frequent job changes are an issue. You can separate the reasons for change from the body of the resume by using italics.

396. Customize your resume for jobs in medicine, government, or academia by beefing up the detail and adding more information. Either have a separate resume or have detailed sections that you can insert as needed.

397. While you usually keep your base resume as generic as possible, making it useful for various disciplines (functional skill sets) and industries, in some cases, you can (and should) use industry buzzwords. Jargon points to your knowledge of the industry and position. In particular, high-tech, oil-and-gas, and banking have a great deal of unique industry language. Using these words in your resume may help get you a toehold, upping your chances of getting an interview. Make your basic resume presentation a bit more generic so hiring managers for other industries and positions can make sense of your background, and then when you're applying for one of the high-buzzword industries, crank up the lingo and insert words in your resume appropriately.

398.

Customize by including publishing kudos. If you have published articles in your industry or functional area, include these in your resume when you are applying for a related position. If you're seeking a general position and the published items make your resume too long, consider deleting them or including them on a separate page or addendum.

399. Customize by adding honors/citations that will help your cause. If you have received honors related to your functional area or industry specialization, include them on your resume. But if you won Den Father of the Year, leave that off and work it into conversation in the interview, if it is relevant.

400. In customizing, weigh whether including military service on your resume will be viewed as a plus. Currently, military service is a definite benefit. If you're applying to work for an organization—a nonprofit, for example—you may consider leaving military experience off your resume. In most cases, though, hiring managers regard military service as a good indication of ability to organize, manage, and team. Also, many people gain valuable technical skills in the armed forces.

401. Decide what to put in and what to leave out by asking, *Would I get hired for this?* This is a good test when you're trying to customize your resume to match specific requirements of the job you're seeking. You may be proud that you are active in your church, but include that in a resume only if you know the reader would be receptive, or if you're applying for a religious position.

402.

Tweak the summary of experience to match the job you're applying for, and make this clear in the cover letter or transmittal that you use to send your resume. If the position calls for a job objective or career goal, prepare several job objectives and career goals and slot them in when needed.

403.

When you customize, steer clear of money talk. Don't volunteer salary or wage information. And if an ad forces the money issue, make a judgment call. If the ad says "salary history required or resume will not be considered," you have two choices: Go ahead and submit your resume without salary information and hope that your background wows the hiring manager enough to grant you an interview. Or provide salary information and follow procedures.

12.

Play up Your Moments of Brilliance

Any employer likes to hire people he or she views as standouts. Show in your resume that you are at the top of your game, or on your way there, and you will probably get your foot in the door. It is not enough just to be competent. Show that you're outstanding. Don't be afraid to brag about yourself.

404. Illustrate the benefit of your work. Show how you not only did your job, but excelled. If you want to succeed in the highly competitive job market, you must document how you made improvements to the position, department, and/or company.

405.

Be specific. Don't just say "reduced employee turnover." Show how you have reduced employee turnover. Use numbers or percentages to prove it.

406. Show that you're excellent. Instead of saying "managed twenty employees well," say: "Found new ways to show employees that they were the company's most important assets by securing for each department head a company car, bonuses, and personal assistant."

407. Underscore how your work helped your employer: "Saved $100,000 by developing and implementing a computer program that automatically calculated interest payments. Saved eight hours per week of employee time from consolidating receiving procedures. Exceeded sales quota by 200 percent in one year by increased prospecting and improved close ratio."

408.
Play up light bulb moments that benefited a company: "Created a program that got new customers' attention—whimsical handouts for sales presentations that kept the company name in front of people."

409. Show instead of tell. One hiring manager tells of a resume-sender who didn't bother to find out the name of the CEO she was writing to, but still made the comment (in the cover letter) "I have all the qualities you're looking for."

410. Watch out for a sentence that misses the boat. A hiring manager offers this example from her file of loser resumes: "My qualifications meet and exceed all your requirements and your CEO won't know what he did without me." Problem was, the CEO was female, and that fact was easily discovered on the website. Does this candidate sound like she's going to meet and exceed requirements if she's not even thorough enough to find out whom she's writing to?

411. Strut your stuff, but don't fluff up your resume by lying about what you have done. Better to list your duties and responsibilities like everyone else than to fib about your background.

412. Make clear what you've done; tell what you added to the group, department, division, company, or corporation. If you've achieved a very technical or complicated goal in information technology, science, or another field, explain your accomplishment in language that a layperson can comprehend. Make sure you have a nontechnical person review your resume.

413.

Take advantage of every opportunity to separate yourself from the herd. A must-include resume item is any praise you have received from customers or bosses on your special talents or abilities. Give this a prominent place in the accomplishments area; don't just tack it on under "personal" items like it's an afterthought.

414.

Pinpoint anything you have done on previous jobs that made you a standout employee. Were you given an award? Did you handle special projects? Did you beef up the company's productivity? Did you save money for a company, thus enhancing the bottom line? In a money-crunch period at the company you worked for, did you assume the responsibilities of two jobs, thus helping to facilitate a reduction in labor force? Spotlight clearly the skills you have that fit the requirements for the position you want.

415.

Don't be shy. Do promote yourself. The race goes to the swift, not the modest.

416. Translate features of your work to benefits. Don't just give a laundry list of what you did in your jobs. Show how things you did (features) benefited the company. This connects the dots for a hiring manager, who wants examples of ways you assisted the company. His chief thought in reading your resume is this: "What can this person do for our company? How will she benefit the bottom line?"

417. Don't say you're a person who "goes the extra mile," if you send a resume, application, and cover letter addressed "To Whom It May Concern." One hiring manager says that's one of her pet peeves. "We had one applicant who sent his application to become our CEO's personal assistant addressed to 'To Whom It May Concern' instead of addressing the CEO by name. This is especially significant because that job ad said that some of the traits our CEO was looking for in an assistant were 'research skills' and 'goes the extra mile.' Finding the CEO's name on our website takes less than a minute of searching, but fewer than 10 percent of applicants bothered to track it down."

418. Let potential employers know that you don't just warm a chair and collect a paycheck, but you have ideas, initiative, and motivation that add up to tangible benefits to the employer. Demonstrate by showing how your efforts always lead to positive benefits for any employer who's smart enough to hire you.

419. Show with numbers. Backing up a claim with numbers is more effective than speaking in general terms. Instead of using the vague "Worked fast and effectively," say, "Decreased by 20 percent the time required to complete loan processing by using effective and efficient work habits."

420. Give dollar amounts. Quantifying your success with dollar amounts is very effective. Instead of saying "Increased sales," say "Increased revenue by $200,000."

421.
Show how you saved time. Accomplishments aren't just about making money or saving money. Saving time counts, too. If you introduced a procedure that cut the time required for a key process by 25 percent, that's important. Saving a company any time at all by streamlining operations and/or training employees to be more efficient should go on your resume because, in the eyes of any hiring manager, this is a big accomplishment.

422. Highlight your extracurricular activities if you've participated in professional or civic activities and served as a leader (officer or member of the board of directors). Leadership experience is especially valuable when you show how it benefited a company. As treasurer of your civic association, you may have reviewed the departmental budget for operational savings. As president of your group, you may have learned management skills that will help you manage people in the workplace. If you handled high-level responsibilities as a volunteer for a nonprofit organization, play up this experience, which can translate to the business world and qualify you for a position with a similar job description.

423. List top accomplishments first on your resume. You don't want the hiring manager to miss these things. If you've just graduated from a university, you list education first, because that's the most important element that a hiring manager will consider when hiring a new grad. If you're an experienced employee campaigning for a certain position, put your accomplishments before duties and responsibilities. In a functional resume or functional/reverse chronological, put the accomplishments up top before listing skills, duties, and responsibilities, or employment history.

424. List company awards and other items that are image building. Make sure your resume showcases your sales award, employee of the week, month, or year, or any other nod to your contributions to the company. Put these achievements in the Accomplishments section of your resume, under the appropriate position.

425.

List as many accomplishments as possible—the more the better, since accomplishments are actually the mainstay of your resume. Many people meet the basic requirements of a position, but hiring managers want people who excel in their jobs. Hopefully, you can list at least two ways you helped a company make money, save money, or save time. If you don't have two accomplishments per position, list one.

426. Translate job duties into accomplishments. Think about what you've done and how you can best describe how you upgraded the company workforce. You have undoubtedly achieved some successes on your jobs, but for some people, translating duties and responsibilities into actual accomplishments is a challenge. You don't have to be the CEO of a Fortune 500 company or a master salesperson to have a litany of credentials that can lead to getting hired. Ponder what you've done for a company that added to its success, and quantify that: "Helped to improve the productivity of the graveyard McDonald's shift to the extent that manager reduced the crew from five to four people."

427. Change a duty to an accomplishment by quantifying the difference made. See how powerful the accomplishment sounds when you compare it to the duty description. Duty: Processed accounts payable for nine retail establishments. Accomplishment: Created a savings of $3,700 on three double-booked invoices by matching purchase order to invoices consistently.

428. Translate management duty to accomplishment. Who would you prefer to hire: the person who just does the day-to-day job, or the person who takes the initiative to improve the way the job is done? Duty: Supervised ten non-exempt employees. Accomplishment: Reduced absenteeism of staff by 20 percent, a $20,000 annual savings in payroll, by implementing flextime schedules for all employees. Allowed employees to pick their day off, which gave employees more control over their schedules, work, and time off, resulting in better morale.

429. Paint a picture. Examples of accomplishments are powerful. Below are a variety of accomplishments that can take your resume a level above your competition. Note that there are some consistencies, no matter what position, industry, or function. You briefly describe your accomplishment and quantify it by using a number, percentage, or dollar increase or decrease. These coups show that you made a difference when you worked for that company—you added value, saved money, made money, or saved time.

Examples include:
- Reengineered processes, functions, and people (including complete replacement of accounting and jobs cost system) to facilitate growth from $285 million to $600 million volume without increasing staff size.

- Rebuilt financial management infrastructure for $600 million service contractor, which resulted in timelier reporting to management and shareholders. Reporting changed from ninety days after year-end to sixty days after year-end, a one-third increase in reporting time.
- Led major system implementation to successful completion in record time.
- Devised and implemented insurance cost recovery methods that yielded $2.5 million per year.
- Negotiated contracts and license agreements, saving 15 percent ($15,000).
- Negotiated vendor discounts of as much as 40 percent.
- Analyzed and improved sales commission structure for increased cost of 8 percent. This resulted in increased motivation in salespeople and a 28 percent increase in sales.
- Worked with partners to increase revenues from $60 million to $300 million.
- Improved, monitored, and recommended company policies and procedures.
- Improved procedures that cut training time 19 percent, resulting in decreased employment cost of $2 million.
- Increased profitability 30 percent through pricing/contract analysis.
- Raised capital and obtained financing; participated in raising more than $20 million in capital.

- Standardized special order worksheet format for the entire company to increase accuracy in processing customized orders.
- Coordinated material returns for warehouses in order to speed posting of adjustments to customer accounts.
- Demonstrated ability to perform independently a variety of duties in departments such as customer service, order entry, computer support, and counter sales.
- Reduced by 20 percent the rollout time for implementation of Oracle G/L module.
- Maintained reporting timetable for company with 10 subsidiaries worldwide, despite severe cuts in accounting personnel.
- Reduced the balance of employee receivable accounts by 23 percent.

430. Ensure that your resume is accomplishment-oriented. Have a friend read it for you and give input.

13.

Put a Positive Spin on Problem Areas

When you're customizing a resume, put a positive spin on areas that might not play in your favor. Any one of the problems listed below has the potential to hold you back, but if you state your case clearly and intelligently, and show the employer that what he may at first perceive as a "drawback" is not going to be a problem for his company, he may give you the chance to prove your mettle.

431. You're overqualified for the job? Make yourself sound flexible, ready to "size down" to the particular job. You can modify your resume to reflect your most recent ten to fifteen years, or five to ten years, of experience. Use the jobs that are most relevant to the position you are seeking.

432. You're out of sync with today's workplace? Show that even though you don't know how to retrieve voice mail, you're a quick study who is willing to learn.

If you lack technical skills in the workplace, be honest and tell the hiring manager that you intend to take classes at a community college or computer training facility. Let them know that you learn quickly and within a short and realistic period of time ("Give me one month and I'll be up to par in technology"). Emphasize your other skills that took years to obtain. Underscore abilities: managerial, project management, and organizational. Convey the idea that while using a word processing program is indeed important, hard-learned skills such as the ones noted above are also valuable.

433. You don't know what people are talking about when they refer to teaming and project management and such? Study today's workplace terms before you write your resume. Hiring managers may say that they don't hold it against anyone when they're unfamiliar with today's keywords or buzzwords, but, in truth, not knowing these things is almost like saying "Computer? What's that?" Even hiring managers who claim to ignore trendy terminology may still have a bit of bias against a candidate who appears to be totally out of the loop ("I don't know what you mean when you refer to formatting skills."). Get ahead of the curve by perusing websites that deal with job searches, and jot down some of the buzzwords used. When you're finished, you'll be ready to write a resume that can hold up in today's keyword-ridden job-search world. It's not OK to be completely out-of-date, no matter what anyone tells you. When you deal with a person who's in the position of hiring people, you're almost always communicating with someone who is on the cutting edge of recruiting lingo, so it's important to show that you are hip to the workforce, too.

434. You had no jobs for years at a time? To make the gaps understandable, you can explain that you're a trust-fund kid, you wrote a book, etc., and your employment sabbaticals don't reflect laziness. Write the explanation on your resume: "Bought 55-foot yacht and sailed the

Caribbean." Hiring managers in many professions appreciate an adventurous spirit. If you're a trust-fund baby, you can list as an employer one of the foundations that your family has, and let that account for the eight years you were jet-setting in Europe and gaining new experiences to write a book, perhaps. (Do this only if you actually had a connection to the foundation!) If you were out of the workforce, just lounging in the sun, be honest. Some employers won't mind. Put your well-written explanation after the last employer, or mention it in your cover letter, too.

435. If the big gaps are there because of unemployment or family problems or considerations, you can modify your resume to reflect your experience in the most favorable manner. These days, many employers are fairly forgiving of gaps in employment, understanding that some economies may dictate longer job searches, and it's less unusual for people to make alternate arrangements to accommodate family needs. You may want to use a reverse chronological format; list your most recent employers and add a line or two describing the reason for the gap: "Left employer to care for ailing relative." You may also want to explain in your cover letter.

436.

Want to omit information? Just don't add information that's incorrect or alter dates. On your resume, you can omit older information from the beginning of your career simply because you don't think it's applicable anymore, but when you fill out an employment application, list complete employment information. An employment application is a legal document; the fine print at the end says that you can be dismissed from the job for falsifying the application. Any job you leave off your resume in an effort to get in the door must be listed on the employment application, in the spirit of full disclosure. This is a strict rule.

437.

Changed careers? Modify your resume to fit the position. For example, let's say you were a postal carrier for fifteen years and then went back to school for your English degree. You can feel free to leave off your postal carrier experience. On the other hand, if you think it will help you get the job, leave it in. Returning to undergraduate school allows you to start the slate with that new degree.

438. Some of your past jobs don't really count toward anything you're looking for? Modify your resume to omit positions that don't apply. You may have worked for a number of years in different positions in one industry or one functional area. Let's say you were a chemical engineer in six different chemical plants in your twenty-year career. The first two jobs you had straight out of engineering school (fourteen and eighteen years ago) don't apply to any job you now want, so just leave them off your resume.

439. Worried you'll be branded a job-hopper? Functional resumes are good for a person who has a disjointed resume full of numerous employers. This format highlights skills and experience and downplays the employers, which is a great way to handle unusual job histories. The catch is that many experienced hiring managers are suspicious of functional resumes; they wonder, *What's wrong with this picture?* That's why it's important to use this approach wisely.

440.

Worried you have few jobs to sell, just skills? That's all right. Use a hybrid; you get the best of both worlds by combining a functional resume and a reverse chronological resume. Put skills and experience at the top (don't forget computer skills and languages). With a hybrid resume, the reader gets a quick picture of what you have to offer. Below the Skills/Experience section, list any employers and duties, and responsibilities performed, to let hiring managers know when and where you honed your skills.

441.

You don't know zip about computers? Explain in your cover letter that you will overcome this deficiency by taking courses, studying at night, etc. If you're returning to the workplace after an absence of five or more years, chances are you may be technologically challenged because the pace in info-technology is rapid. Even six months is a long time to be out of touch. Whether you're an IT specialist or you simply use information technology, get up to speed as quickly as possible. Don't just wring your hands. Take a class, borrow a computer, and learn the skills you need. Requirements vary from company to company, but basic computer literacy dictates knowledge of Microsoft products Windows, Word, and

Excel. Computer programs are built similarly, so once you learn Excel, you can learn Lotus 123. Once you learn Word, you can learn WordPerfect. While the idea of mastering new areas may seem daunting, just resolve to do what you need to do. You will be at a huge disadvantage if you go to an employer without this basic knowledge under your belt.

442. You have a disability? Clarify how you can compensate if the challenge will matter in performing the job. Under the 1990 Americans with Disabilities Act, an employer has the responsibility to determine if you can do the job at hand with "reasonable accommodation." That means that if you're in a wheelchair, the employer widens the door and modifies your desk. However, if you're wheelchair-bound and apply for a job climbing poles for the phone company, reasonable accommodation is impossible, so you can legally be denied the job. If you're deaf and you apply for a telemarketing job, the company cannot provide reasonable accommodation to make this position feasible for you, but you could handle an accounts payable job with reasonable accommodation. You don't have to disclose disabilities that aren't obvious if you know you can do a certain job without reasonable accommodation.

443. You have a spotty marital history? The fact that you are marriage-challenged is no one's business. According to the Civil Rights Act of 1967, marital status can't be used as a consideration in hiring. Don't ask. Don't tell. If you've made significant job changes or geographic moves because of divorce, you actually have valid reasons for changing jobs, but you still shouldn't feel compelled to explain that marriage splits caused the disruptions in work. Putting marital status and children on your resume is a relic of yester-year. Some people list this information because they think that being "married, with children" makes them look more established. Wrong. It's just not a factor.

444. You've been arrested? Don't adver-tise this in your resume. If you have been arrested but not convicted, you don't need to tell a hiring manager—ever. An employment appli-cation usually asks, "Have you ever been convicted of a crime?" One reason that hiring managers shouldn't factor arrests into their decisions is that, statistically, minorities are more often arrested. As a job-hunting individual, you need to know your legal rights, and one of these is that you are not required to bring up arrests that didn't result in convictions, or instances of deferred adjudication if these have already been cleared from your record.

445. You've been arrested and convicted? The key word is "and" in arrested and convicted. If you have been arrested and convicted of a criminal offense, you have some explaining to do. Remember, an employer can easily run a criminal check on your background; in fact, that's usually the first background check done. When you do broach the subject of your felony, keep your comments brief and to the point, the same way you would explain a bad job or a firing. Don't laugh it off or act unrepentant. Tell what happened and add that you have paid your debt to society and learned your lesson. Mention to the hiring manager that if he gives you a chance, you'll make him glad he did (and then do exactly that).

446.

You have alcohol/drug abuse in your past? Don't address this issue in your resume unless that problem accounts for periods of unemployment. If so, you can attribute the work gap to "an illness that is no longer a problem." Basically, your past is past, and if you can do the job you're applying for, that's all you're required to tell a company representative.

447. You've undergone extensive therapy? Don't reveal this in your resume or during an interview. It's not smart to brag about therapy. Restrain yourself from sharing your therapy history or milestones. Don't deal in psychobabble or talk about how much you have grown as a person through therapy. Unless your hiring manager is one of the enlightened few, a disclosure of mental problems may kill your chances of getting a job. You can, however, use the interview time to show what you've learned about people and how that makes you a skillful, insightful manager and/or employee. Take what you have learned in therapy and couch it in business terms. Knowing yourself and understanding those around you will make you a more valuable employee.

448. You have four young children? Don't flaunt this on a resume. You absolutely do not need to list children, their names, their ages. Being a parent doesn't make you more or less qualified for a job. The exception is if you're seeking a job in education. If you think having children is a plus in teaching, counseling, or management, tell the hiring manager during your interview.

Some employers don't view being a parent as an asset (especially if you're a mother). An old-fashioned prejudice says that mothers take off work when their children are sick or have school programs and conferences. Even though today's parents often share kid responsibilities, many employers still regard rearing children as a "mother issue." At any rate, showing up is the most basic part of working, and because of that, some employers automatically shy away from someone with major-league childcare responsibilities. If an interviewer asks if you have children—an illegal question, by the way—sidestep the question and talk about your excellent attendance record and ability to work the required hours.

Of course, sidestepping the question may annoy a hiring manager, who presumes you're being evasive because you have something awful to hide. Sometimes, it may seem that you'd be better off revealing the fact that you have twelve children. This is a damned-if-you-do and damned-if-you-don't situation; if you're meeting with a hiring manager who is biased against employees with kids, you will suffer in comparison to a childless candidate. At the same time, there's a lot to be said for the truth. (After all, if you are hired, you won't be able to keep your big brood a secret.)

449. You've had the same job for a hundred years? Some hiring managers view spending too long in the same position as a red flag. Maybe you weren't promoted because you weren't a standout or you lacked initiative, or maybe you're lazy and don't mind a dead-end job. These misconceptions can be as detrimental to your job search as jumping to a new job every two months. How do you handle the fact that you've had one job for the past twenty-five years? On your resume, break the job up into a series of projects, using sub-positions just as you would different positions in the same company. Use different projects, duties, and responsibilities to split up the job into two-year increments. List dates and different positions, and show your progression in the company. What you want to illustrate is that you did grow, even though the name of the position never changed.

450. You've worked for the same company your whole career? Address this in your resume. America is all about change. No one wants you to change companies too often, but no one likes it when you stay at the same company your entire career, either. If you change companies too often, some folks will dismiss you as a job-hopper (and hiring managers may think you're disloyal). If you stay at the same company your entire career, you could be viewed as lacking ambition, stale, or limited (knowing only one way to do things). On your resume, meet this question head-on by listing various positions you had in the company; show how you soared. Tweak your experience at that company in a positive way so that hiring managers won't jump to negative conclusions. Anticipate the bias, and put your own spin on it.

451. You're working your way down the corporate ladder? Show on your resume that it's not because your employers hated you or thought you were incompetent. You want a less demanding job because you've had a change in lifestyle; you're paring down; you had a baby or adopted a child. Or maybe the downward spiral just reflects a change in attitude; you want to back off on that workaholic reputation. In growing older, some people no longer want to struggle up the corporate ladder and prefer more time for family, exercise, travel, and just plain fun. Or maybe this trend in your jobs simply reflects a slow economy that forced you to take the best job available at the time. No matter. You can use interview time to state honestly your reason for taking a job that was "beneath" you. If you think that your chance of getting an interview would be improved by covering this matter up front, explain your reasons for job change in your resume or cover letter. But keep your explanation upbeat. You don't want to show an attitude of "poor me" or "I'm so unlucky." No company wants to hire a self-described loser.

452. Years of self-employment? If you've had your own business for more than five years or have been self-employed for a long time, employers may have doubts about your background and qualifications. Granted, it's not fair, but they may indeed discount the work you have done on your own. Typically, owning a small business or working as a self-employed contractor teaches a multitude of skills that can be used in the work world. You learn about the product or service provided, plus finance, accounting, operations, management, leasing, and many other facets of business. If you're this kind of businesswoman or self-employed guy, face the challenge of conveying and translating your experience to the potential employer. Include quantifiable accomplishments, not just a laundry list of claims.

453.

Your work experience was overseas? Explain how this translates in the U.S.

If you worked overseas for five or more years, you may find yourself explaining to your potential employers about the nature of your work, especially if you did work that was specific to the country, such as accounting or legal work. Your task on a resume is to correlate the work that you did overseas to comparable tasks in the United States.

454. You've done contract jobs on the side while you worked full time? Explain this carefully. As long as there haven't been conflicts of interest, you may want to highlight contract experience that complemented your full time work. The best way to accomplish that and not confuse the reader is to list the contract work below your full time work and point out that the contract work was done part-time while you worked at your full time position. Make it clear that you didn't use time at your full time job to perform other job tasks in a covert manner (you don't want to come across as sneaky).

455. Your resume is as long as a book? Fix it. If you've had numerous jobs, you'll have a four-page resume unless you resist the urge to recap every job and responsibility you've had. A hiring manager focuses on your most recent three to five years of experience (or one year if you are in info technology or a fast-moving science field). You need to truncate those jobs from 20 years ago, or omit them.

456. You've had five jobs in four years in the same position? Spin this point. Frequent job changes may hurt you in some professions, especially the stuffier ones. Here's the best approach: Group all the similar jobs under one heading, and use a date from the first job to the last job.

457. You're a Ph.D. who wants a B.A. job? Edit your resume with that in mind. If you are overeducated for a position you're seeking, leave the advanced degree off the resume. There's nothing wrong with doing that, and it may help you get a job. If it comes up later, after you're hired, you can always say that you didn't consider the Ph.D. relevant because this particular job didn't require a Ph.D.

458.

You've spent the last six years doing work you didn't want to do? Show on your resume that you want to return to the kind of work you did before your current job. Even if you have gotten into work that you don't enjoy and have kept doing it, you're not necessarily stuck. Just prepare a functional resume that reinforces the work you did previously and underplays the work you're no longer interested in. Play up the right part, and the hiring manager won't focus on the "nothing" job that you hate.

459. You have a scary hobby? Leave it off your resume. If your hobby is sky-diving, bungee-jumping, or body piercing, share that with friends, but leave risk-taking endeavors off your resume. Also, don't talk about extreme sports during interviews. Unless you're applying for a job as a racecar driver, test pilot, or some other job where daring is an asset, don't mention risky hobbies or wild ways.

460. You were educated in another country? Use your resume to translate that education for the U.S. yardstick. Someone educated overseas may find that his education isn't totally applicable to United States programs. Your best bet is to list comparable courses taken or hours completed and show work experience that's top-notch.

461. Don't be surprised if hiring managers view your education in another country as a "not-our-problem" issue. It's your job to spin this issue in a positive way.

It's a good idea to go to a local university and have your college credits from South Africa translated to U.S. standards so that employers can assess exactly where you stand for hiring purposes. Use your cover letter to explain this translation of your hours completed at an overseas university. Or just emphasize the skills you have and not the college courses you took. Don't expect a prospective employer to take on the work of making your foreign education understandable on U.S. turf.

462. You were a teacher before getting your M.B.A.? Use this as a point in your favor. If you worked in a completely different discipline before getting your master's degree, this fact can be a big plus. If you were a music teacher for ten years and then decided to get your master's in mathematics, use the combination of creativity and attention to detail from music and apply it to math.

463.

You're able to do a job requiring a degree but don't have one? In this instance, you want to show that your experience matters greatly. Three years of practical experience can compensate for each year of experience required with a degree. Put major emphasis on ways in which your work experience makes you qualified for the job.

464. You've worked for a huge corporation, but no one can tell what you've done because the work sounds esoteric? Use your resume to make your job tasks sound generic. Acronyms and specialized internal titles or functions are OK if you're dealing with internal personnel, but if you're looking for a job, you want the person on the street to be able to understand what you've done. If you don't make sense of your resume, no one else will. Hiring managers won't stop to interpret confusing or obtuse resumes. Instead, they just turn to another in the big stack of resumes and leave yours behind.

For example, if you were called a "purveyor of sensitive information," explain what that means in the real world: Did you handle top-secret documents? Did you have a high-level clearance that meant you were a decision-maker? What were you doing for those two years?

465. You work for a secret agency and can't disclose information? Then translate the skills you use. No hiring manager wants you to get killed for divulging top-secret documents, but you must be able to show experience that applies to the position you want. Don't expect a hiring manager to be a mind reader just because you've been a covert operative. If you're discreet and diplomatic enough to warrant a top-secret job, you obviously possess the skills to translate what you have done into generic enough language that you won't end up in Leavenworth.

466. You've been in prison? While it's hard to disguise those four-year gaps in your resume, don't list on your resume "spent four years incarcerated." That takes honesty to a counterproductive level. Using a functional resume format, list skills, experience, and accomplishments. Then, during the interview, tell the truth when the hiring manager asks you to explain the gaps. (Many companies do background checks anyway.) If you can convince the employer that you have been rehabilitated, you have a better chance of getting and keeping a job than if you lie and are found out. Say that you're now on the right track, and be sincere and straightforward, not devious and secretive. Some employers pride themselves on giving ex-cons second chances.

467. You worked for a company that disappeared in a public disgrace? Handle this issue with care. If the company is several years down on your resume, your biggest problem will be hearing a few bad jokes. But if you worked there when the company imploded, the employer you're interviewing with will either run the other way just because you're from that unsavory company, or he might think of you as a tough guy because you survived a difficult environment and stuck it out to the end. Most supervisors like tenacious employees. Handling adversity well is usually considered a plus.

468. You've changed your name numerous times through marriages/divorces and you wonder how your resume should reflect this information? Employers often track down references from companies far in your working past—and this is especially true if a hiring manager knows someone from a previous company where you worked—but you don't need to go through your litany of name changes until you reach the reference stage. Then, list on the reference page the name that the reference will recognize. During the interview, respond honestly when the hiring manager asks for the scoop on your aliases. Lots of people have former marriages, and usually no one will hold this against you. However, be realistic enough to understand that you face the hiring manager's personal bias concerning divorce, and that's something you can't predict or control.

14.

Snag Those Letters of Recommendation and References

When you work for a company, keep the notion of getting good references in the back of your mind, and it will make you a better employee. When you need a great letter of recommendation, you will have a willing donor. When you leave a job, it's smart to clear up all loose ends before you depart. Finish your work and then some, and try to leave everyone with a good feeling about your having worked there.

Eventually, in seeking a job, you will be asked for references; thus, you must be prepared to hand these over. Here are some things you need to know about references and letters of recommendation:

469. Remember that work references mean much more than personal references. Sure, your sister thinks you're very cool, but what about your last boss? Try to view your list of references the way you would look at it if you were hiring someone. Include ones that pack a power punch.

470. Don't paperclip, staple, or glue letters of recommendation to your resume.

471.
Don't put the words "references available" on your resume. You can omit a mention of references altogether or include a sentence in your cover letter: "I can provide excellent references on request." By the way, most employers assume that anyone who is looking for a job has a list of references.

472. Choose people who make good references. Don't list someone who is stingy with praise or anyone who represents a job you had eight or more years ago. The fact that you did a good job back when you sold popcorn at a theatre when you were sixteen is only mention-worthy if you're twenty-two or younger. Find a supervisor who can attest to those skills that make you stand out from the crowd of job-searchers. If you choose a supervisor who thinks you were great at your ditch-digging job during the summers of your college years, you run the risk of coming across as someone very desperate for a reference.

473. Choose people who can talk. The boss who spoke in monosyllables probably won't do you any favors. Don't list anyone who won't be complimentary or forthcoming (even though he liked you). These days, a hiring manager often interprets a "no comment" as a negative. He may suspect that this supervisor didn't like you but refuses to say so in a time of hyper-litigious employees.

474. Ask your choices if they will serve as references. It's bad etiquette to put someone down on your list of references without checking first to see if it's OK. This approach also protects your own best interests; that way, if you want to list a supervisor you thought approved of your performance but who actually did not, he has a way out: "I don't do references." If you list him without asking, he may respond with a possibly damaging "no comment" or reveal the truth—that you were a so-so employee, in his opinion. A reluctant reference is worse than no reference at all.

475.
Look for an enthusiastic reference—someone who is always quick to issue praise generously. Don't expect your creepy old boss Drab Don to turn into a great reference, wildly effusing about you, when he has never been excited about anything in his entire life. Be realistic about your chances.

476. Don't underestimate the importance of good references. Make sure that you have three to five references from past employers. Some companies want personal references, but usually the best references are direct supervisors and people who have seen your work on a first-hand basis. Second best: your boss's boss. Third best: people who reported directly to you.

477. Don't include references in resumes. If someone requests references in the initial resume submission process, and you are asked to include supervisors who you know won't give you a thumbs-up, weigh the advantages versus the disadvantages of sending them. (You know whether you're going to get resoundingly strong endorsements—or not.) At any rate, hiring managers rarely contact references until a candidate has interviewed at least once.

478. List as a reference a boss who praised your performance, not just any old boss.

479. Choose a well-spoken reference. If a reference of yours clams up, the hiring manager may jump to the conclusion that he's withholding bad news because he fears legal repercussions.

480. Don't list a former supervisor who will not return phone calls or answer mail or email. If you have a good reference no one can reach, it won't do you much good. You worked there; you know who the tough-to-reach non-communicators are, so steer clear of listing them and wasting the hiring manager's time.

481. Include on your list of references a boss from your most recent years of employment. If you have no one to list from those recent jobs, move down the totem pole and search your colleagues for someone who worked with you and can say something good about you. That's better than listing a supervisor who can't think of a single thing he liked about you.

482. Make your list of references a separate entity from your resume. Your list of references should be a sheet that you take with you to an interview. And don't forget to carry some extras; the individual who goes on an interview without an up-to-date list of references may raise eyebrows. The hiring manager wonders, How prepared can this applicant be on-the-job if he can't even remember to bring key items to an important interview?

483.

Follow proper etiquette and offer references when asked. Otherwise, don't bring them up, and don't wave your list in the interviewer's face and insist that he take it. Being pushy doesn't usually merit a check in the plus column.

484.

Make sure the contact information on each reference person is complete and up-to-date. Failure to bother with this is a common mistake, according to hiring managers and headhunters. In a rush to get your job hunt cranking, you pull out an old list of references and fail to update it even though you know that some of the numbers or addresses aren't current. (This is especially true in this time of changing cell numbers and email addresses.)

Remember that failure to update your reference list makes you look lazy and slipshod. You say that you want the hiring manager to believe you're capable and thorough, but you let your very first encounter with him send a different message—that you're not thorough enough to update your reference list.

485.

If you do not list your most recent supervisor, an interviewer may ask you why not during an interview, so it's smart to prepare an answer just in case that comes up. If you explain that you and your supervisor didn't see eye to eye, don't launch a long diatribe on what a creep he was and how he didn't appreciate you, and so on. The hiring manager can easily imagine himself in the position of the maligned former supervisor. That won't help you get the job.

486.
Don't include letters of recommendation with your resume. You can hand them over during an interview. These are viewed as "initial references," and usually an employer asks for additional references because unfavorable letters of recommendation are nonexistent. If someone gave you a bad one, would you flash it before the eyes of hiring managers? It's similar to a plastic surgeon showing prospective patients sets of before-and-after pictures of patients who were satisfied with their surgical results, but where are the photos of average cases and below average?

487. Don't list a gossip or a too-talkative reference. What if he spills the story about that time you acted freaky at work? You don't want a hiring manager to know about the day you had a psychotic episode during a deadline, or when you missed a month because your divorce depressed you. In our litigious society, you probably figure no one would ever air your dirty laundry—and you may be right—but it still happens, so why risk exposure?

488. Understand that most companies rely on the verbal testimonials of those who had direct contact with you—prior supervisors, peers, or subordinates with whom you worked. Letters of recommendation are only a formality, which means they get 10 percent credibility. One headhunter explains, "We know that people get their best friends to write letters of recommendation, and even O.J. or Ted Bundy could find someone to say he was a good guy. Needless to say, this is why letters of recommendation get merely a quick glance; few hiring managers or headhunters take them seriously."

489. Don't forget about the downside of listing a job that has a bad story attached to it. If your job history will lead a hiring manager to a boss who wants to ruin you, omit that job altogether from your resume. True, you may have to explain the "hole" in your record ("What were you doing for a living from 1984 to 1999?"), but that's probably easier than trying to explain away the comments of a supervisor who decides to spill his memories of Least Favorite Employee of the Year: "R. J. Dolittle never called in when he was going to miss work. He came in late and left early every day. He was sick ten times a month. His coworkers stayed mad at him half the time because they got stuck doing his job. Don't hire him!"

There's no straighter route to the trash can for your resume than an awful reference; even a mediocre one can put you out of contention for a job because you're probably going up against people with good references.

490.

If you are currently employed, make sure you perform your current job in a way that will guarantee you a good reference. Deliver what employers consider an ethical performance—a full day of productive work.

491. When you quit a job, scout out a couple of coworkers who would make good references. An example would be someone you have worked closely with who thinks your work is outstanding—or who knows that you complete your work in a timely manner, or who thinks you are smart and clever.

492.
Occasionally ask for feedback from a supervisor when you are new on a job. And, if possible, try to get something in writing. Then, if you are ever hard pressed for a good reference, you can pull out that complimentary email or note. You may be able to get some kind words more easily during the early months of a job when supervisors are eager to hand out compliments because they want to motivate you.

493. If someone refuses to be a reference for you, look at this as a great opportunity to learn something about yourself as an employee. You probably won't like hearing the bad news, but, at the same time, this can be a road toward self-improvement. Listen to what this individual says—and use it.

For example, let's say that the supervisor who won't serve as a reference tells you that every time he offered constructive criticism, you bristled and argued. Not once would you actually listen and try to upgrade your work. Does that sound like an open-minded employee who is willing to learn and grow?

Of course, no one relishes criticism; the words can sting. But, you won't improve if you never discover why you're not the one who gets raises or promotions. Summon up the gutsiness to turn a disappointing moment around; when a boss says, "I'd rather not be listed as one of your references," ask, "Would you mind sharing with me the reason behind that decision? I would like to become a better employee." Make your words heartfelt and few employers will refuse to answer your question.

You may be surprised. Sometimes bosses view you as weak in areas in which you think you're strong and vice versa. Knowledge is power. When you know how you are being perceived, you may be able to turn the situation around.

Most of us can't see ourselves the way others see us in the workplace, home, or anyplace else for that matter. But if you're an employee who rarely gets praise from a supervisor or coworker, something's wrong. You could use some soul-searching—that is, if you want to grow.

494. If you have a book or portfolio that includes letters of recommendation, keep tabs on how they look. Headhunters and hiring managers tell horror stories of receiving letters of recommendation on paper so old that it was wrinkled and yellow. This makes you look like someone who doesn't update his or her "package" and whose letters of recommendation are so ancient the people who wrote them are probably dead. That may not be the case, but that's the impression you give, and job-hunting is an impression-based business. Work with it—not against it. Even the carrying case for your portfolio is important because it sends a design statement. A hiring manager will rate your case just like he rates the clothes you wear on an interview. Buy a case that fits the materials you want to display and that isn't too heavy. You can't go wrong with a zippered presentation case.

495. When you call to make sure a hiring manager received your resume, don't mention your letters of recommendation, and don't quote people on your reference list. This turns off busy people. After you ask, "Is this a good time for you?" keep the call short and businesslike. The hiring manager doesn't want to hear a sales pitch, but he probably will confirm that he received your resume. Don't be intrusive or pushy. That will count against you as much as wearing jeans to an interview. It *is* possible to talk yourself out of a job.

496. Don't presume that a hiring manager wants to hear you brag. Wait to be asked. And, hopefully, you can do your touting via a list of strong references who will speak on your behalf.

497. Check everything on your reference list. Make sure there are no typos or smudged type or a printout that's so light it's hard to read.

498.
If there's something about your life that you don't want advertised, advise the people on your reference list who know about it. They may not know to keep quiet about the fact that you have ten children and another on the way.

499. Don't forget that there are possibilities for references outside your immediate supervisor and coworkers—those people who have worked with you in ex-officio ways. Examples are trade organizations, clients, and such.

500. If you get someone's permission to list him as a reference—but you still have qualms about what he will say about you—get a friend to make a call, pretending to be an employer who wants to know about your job record/history. Take no chances that you've listed someone who will make negative or nothing comments, thus ending your likelihood of getting an interview. If in doubt, check it out. You have nothing to lose by exercising a little paranoia.

501.

Give every reference a copy of your resume so that that person has information on the dates and places you worked. Don't make your reference have to do the homework. Few people can remember exactly when you worked for the company or how long. What they do remember is the kind of employee you were.

502. Provide anyone who agrees to be a reference with a short list of qualities/traits that you think are your strengths. If you list industriousness, point out that you volunteered often for extra assignments. If you list creativity, cite projects that you came up with and how these impacted the company's bottom line. If you list leadership, recap your positions of authority and how these led to more promotions. This refreshes the memory of your reference and makes him better able to help you. (Typically, if someone agrees to be a reference, he's interested in furthering your cause.)

503. If you know that certain traits are of special interest to a company, inform your reference and ask him to emphasize the particular trait. If you're applying for a money-handling job or one that involves proprietary information, you need someone to vouch for you as a trustworthy, ethical person whose character is beyond reproach.

504. If you know that your reference is extremely busy (and unlikely to deliver the required information), offer to prepare a letter for his or her signature. Explain that you would be glad to do a rough draft. Some people jump at this chance.

505.

Before you vacate your cubicle for good, ask for a letter of recommendation from your supervisor. If he or she refuses (or isn't available), get a coworker or subordinate to write one for you.

506.

If a bad reference keeps rearing its ugly head, find that person and apologize for the blowup that occurred when you were fired—or the day you sliced up her car tires—or the hot-head moment when you were forced to resign. Try to exert damage control, clean up the mess you left, and move on. Tell this reference that you're not asking for a good reference, only a neutral one.

507.

If an old boss insists on ruining your chances of getting a new job, hire a lawyer to write a letter threatening legal action. Disparaging you can be construed as libel (if it's written) or slander (if it's spoken), and most companies frown on supervisors whose actions lead to nasty litigation.

508.

Don't make the mistake of thinking that bad references from former bosses can't hurt you. These are land mines. That's why you must do anything you can to make amends for any "burned bridges." Sure, you got mad and lost your temper and said things you shouldn't have, but even creepy supervisors from your past have hearts. Try to patch things up so that the ghosts of jobs past won't haunt you.

15.

Show Appreciation for Resume Help Without Fawning

Thanking people who help you in your job search is a way to cultivate stronger relationships, keep your name out in front of more people, and show that you have social and business skills.

Consider the advertising concept called TOMA, Top-of-the-Mind Awareness. This means that the more often and the more recently you've heard a name, the more likely you are to remember it and buy it. Because your resume is a marketing tool, you want to make sure you get your name out there and make it easy for someone to hire you. Sending thank-you notes helps. You've involved many people in your job search, from recruiters to reference-givers to friends who proof your resume, and you need to thank them all.

Tips for showing your appreciation include:

509. Remember to say thank you. Saying thank you is one of the most underestimated and underrated of social and business graces. It can mean the difference between getting a job or not.

510. Choose your salutation carefully. Should you use a first name or a salutation such as Ms., Mr., or Mrs.? It depends on your relationship with the person. In the United States, we are often informal with business contacts. If someone is introduced to you as Mrs. Executive and she never asks you to use her first name, start the thank-you note with the salutation and her last name: Dear Mrs. Executive. Otherwise, address business contacts by their first names.

511.

Don't be overly effusive in thanking an interviewer to the point that it makes you seem needy or weird. The best idea: Express thanks when you're leaving the interview room, and then go home and write a note to mail the same day.

512. Don't send gifts or flowers to a hiring manager who interviewed you because it looks like payola (I'm giving you a present so you'll feel obligated to hire me). You can, however, send flowers to your recruiter. Just make sure you don't send flowers or gifts to say thank you for interviewing or to ingratiate yourself with a hiring manager; it may be construed as a minor bribe.

513. Express appreciation to recruiters, references, and friends who encourage you in your job search. Your benefactor may speak up on your behalf again in the future.

514. Send a monthly or quarterly update on your job search to your database of friends, family, business acquaintances, and general acquaintances. Let them know what kinds of leads you want to hear about as you continue to look for a job.

515.

Send thank-you notes to every person who interviews you. Lots of job candidates don't think it's necessary to write to every single person they talked to during an interview. They speculate that they won't be able to figure what to say on six different thank–you notes, and what if one interviewer compares her note to the one another interviewer received? That doesn't matter. What's important is that it's smart to write each interviewer a note! In some cases, this small token of good manners decides who gets the job. Even if you were phone-interviewed by four individuals, get all of the names before you hang up, including their positions, and send a special note to each person.

516.

Write a thank-you note by hand unless your handwriting is illegible. Most employers and hiring managers think handwritten thank-you notes are best, but if your writing is impossible to read, type it. Remember that the handwritten note stands out because it won't be in a standard, business-size number-ten envelope. This means it gets opened first.

517. If you're going on lots of interviews and can't stand the idea of writing multiple thank-you notes, it may be easier to use a computer-generated thank-you note that you can customize for each individual. The basic rule behind notes of appreciation is to do them. Whether they appear in nice handwriting on lovely note cards or typed on bond paper, the important thing is that you remember.

518. Email your thank-you note if the hiring decision is going to be made within forty-eight hours—or if email is so standard in your functional area that using the U.S. postal system would make you look old-fashioned and technically challenged.

519. Don't use email just because you're too lazy to write out cards and envelopes. Your potential employer plans to invest a great deal in you (wages, bonuses, benefits, training) so he expects you to invest some time and first-class stamps in your job pursuit.

520.

Use humor in your thank-you note if you're funny. Everyone enjoys a little levity. Plus, a clever statement may make you stand out. If you have something to say that you know will be amusing to the reader, go ahead and try it.

521.

Absolutely do not make any racist, sexist, or religious comments in any correspondence to potential employers. Never include a put-down or disparagement of any group or individual, even in jest; that won't net you any points in the job competition.

522.

If you see an article that applies to the industry or company you've interviewed with, email the article to the person you met. However, make sure the article contains nothing that affects the company negatively. A resume and other communications are about selling yourself, your skills, and your ability to create positive changes for the company. Whether you're vying for CEO or mail room letter-sorter, you get hired for what you can do for the company to improve its operations.

523. Be specific in thank-you notes. Some people use a generic note in which they profusely thank interviewers for their time, state their interest in the company and the position, and assert that they are qualified. But that's dismissed because everyone says the same things. Instead, customize your thank-you note to reflect some specific idea or issue that you recall from the interview. If you discussed a problem that you think you could solve, mention that. Add substance to your note of appreciation.

524. Use cover-letter writing techniques in your thank-you notes. (See chapter 21.)

525.

In your thank-you note, give a reminder that you are an ideal candidate by reiterating the skills you have that make you worthy of serious consideration for this job. Assume that the hiring manager is wavering, trying to decide whom he liked best of those who were interviewed, and this note is your chance to tip the balance in your favor.

526. Use bullet points to list require-ments of the position and match those to your qualifications. This is an effective way to remind the hiring manager that you're a strong candidate for the job.

527. Show interest by calling to follow up on the interview process. During your interview, ask about the hiring steps and when candidates will be contacted regarding interview status. If the hiring manager says one week, wait a week for a call. If you haven't heard from anyone after five business days, call on the sixth day and say that you just want to touch base and see if there is any news; keep the conversation short and to the point, not chatty.

528.
Call if you have an information update: your new cell phone, address, or other pertinent informa-tion. (Any change gives you a good reason to call.)

529. Thanking recruiters can build relationships. Recruiters are paid to help people find jobs. Some work on a retained (retainer) basis, others on contingency. Retained means they get paid whether they produce the winning candidate or not. Contingency means they get paid only if they are successful in producing a candidate who is hired; these recruiters work primarily in executive levels and very specific job niches. Translated, this means your recruiter may or may not realize any financial gain from working with you. And just like any business relationship, you're building rapport with your recruiter. If that person likes you and believes in you, he can lead you to many jobs.

530.

Thank your references. It takes fifteen to forty-five minutes to give a reference; and any reference may contribute a slot of valuable time to help with your job search. Return the favor by thanking each person on your list.

531. Thank friends who were kind enough to help with resume proofing and all of those friends and family members who have helped in your job search. Do so soon after their assistance. Send a handwritten note unless your writing is illegible—then, type a note. The most casual and least sincere way to send a thank-you note to a friend who helped in your job search is to shoot her an email. Email is a great way to communicate, and it's an incredibly easy way to send a message, but when you want to express appreciation to someone for his extra effort on your behalf, send a handwritten note.

532. For most people who help you, thank-you flowers, pecan pies, and fruit baskets would be overkill, but you can send a small pamphlet, brochure, or small book—anything that can fit in a number-ten envelope, or even an 8x11-inch envelope. For family members who help, anything goes—flowers, gifts, or treats.

533. Use common sense in following up with a business acquaintance. Don't look desperate or cloying.

534. Show that you mean it. Your reader has probably seen his or her share of thank-you notes, so take the time to make the note sincere and fresh. Express how much you appreciate the effort on your behalf. Although people like to help each other, most also want to know that their efforts are appreciated. Be friendly and warm if that's natural, especially if you're writing to a close friend.

535. If you had a techie friend or business associate review your resume, mention the technical additions or clarifications that person added.

536.
Use conservative stationery. For an acquaintance who has done you a good turn, use a plain note card. Don't buy greeting cards that say "Thank you" on the top flap or similar note cards. A high-quality, plain note card looks distinctive and professional.

537. Don't send a thank-you note if the person who assisted you in reviewing or preparing your resume works in an organization that frowns on personal correspondence. If you know the person well enough, send the thank-you to her home address.

538. If you've interviewed for a position that's confidential, ask the interviewer if it is appropriate for her to receive a thank-you note. You don't want to jeopardize the confidentiality of the search.

539. Send thanks even if you decide you don't want the job. Perhaps going on the interview changed your mind, or you've discovered something about the company that bothers you. At any rate, using good manners is always a good idea. You may change your mind again about that position after you've gone down the road a bit. Show appreciation for the effort the interviewer made, whether the results were what you expected or not. You'll never regret having done something nice.

540. Remember that timing can be a pivotal element of a job search. If you're sending a handwritten note, put it in the mail within twenty-four hours of your interview. If you're sending a computer-written note via mail, send it within twenty-four hours. An email communication should go out within forty-eight hours. You have more leeway with email because your reader gets the note almost immediately. Although the hirer may not read your email the same day you send it, you'll make a good impression by sending it very soon after your interview. Some consultants tell job-search candidates to wait seven to ten days before sending thank-you notes, but that's a bad idea considering current attention spans because you run the risk that the hiring manager may have forgotten you by then. Wait too long to express thanks and you may find that the job was filled by the time you stuck a stamp on your tardy thank-you note.

541.

Ask your references to send notes of affirmation to your interviewers. Nothing helps as much as outside endorsements, even if they are not totally unbiased. If you think you're close to landing a job, call two references and ask them to email a few words of endorsement to your future employer. That way, the interviewer gets some outside words on how fabulous you are.

542. Thank by phone as a second choice. Phoning a friend who helped you in the interview process or calling a hiring manager isn't a bad idea, but remember, you want to show that you put some effort into your thanks. Picking up the phone is the fastest and easiest way to thank someone, and, of course, writing takes longer. If you have no other way to reach someone you need to thank, use the phone. But when the person gets on the line, immediately ask "Is this a good time for you?" so that he has a way to bail out if you've called at an inconvenient time. You don't want to express your thanks and annoy the hiring manager at the same time. Ponder the wisdom of calling; you want to make sure that you're not going to be a pest. If you noticed during your interview that the interviewer was a "hurry-hurry", "I'm-so-stressed" type, don't call at all. That kind of supervisor won't appreciate a phone overture and may chalk it up as a negative.

543. Don't get too cute. You want to show appreciation to people who helped you with your resume or interviewed you. Absolutely. But unless you're in entertainment or advertising, don't send singing telegrams, strippers, etc. (This has happened!)

544. Whether you're handwriting a letter or using the computer, spell correctly and use good grammar. When you write something down, it's there in black-and-white, forever open to scrutiny. For many hiring managers, a spelling or grammatical error will be glaringly apparent (and bothersome).

545. Spell every name correctly. Everyone's favorite word is his or her name. Misspell it in writing and you have lost an ally. When in doubt, call the organization or the person to verify the spelling. Attention to detail makes a big difference in the way you are perceived.

546.
Don't flirt when thanking an interviewer. He may think you're coming on to him.

547. You may hand-deliver your thank you the same day you interviewed, but don't try to initiate a chat while you're there. Be considerate of the supervisor's time and just drop off the note you've written.

16.

Get Your Resume into the Right Hands

The most ingenious, accomplishment-laden resume is nothing but words on a piece of paper unless it gets into the right hands—those of someone who can hire you or direct you toward the person who can. That's why a key element of the job search is finding out whose name should be on the envelope when you send a resume.

Follow the instructions in the job listing, but try to find out what the F. in F. Higgins stands for, and his position, too. You want to send your resume to a real, live person, not just Director of Personnel or

Human Resources Director, which can be a dead-end road.

Here are tips for making sure your resume lands in the hands that wield the hiring power:

548.
Find out the name of the person on the receiving end. If you have the correct name of the hiring manager and use it to address your resume cover letter and envelope, this improves your chances of having that person actually receive your resume and look at it. Almost everyone will read a piece of mail with his name on it, especially when that name is spelled correctly and followed by the correct title.

549.
Realize what can happen to a resume with a cover letter saying "to whom it may concern." To human resources personnel, this means that you didn't bother to get the name of the resume recipient. Of course, your resume may make it through the maze anyway, and someone may even read it, but then again, maybe not. If you don't use the name of the person who does the hiring, don't expect mail room or departmental personnel to route your envelope to the proper person. Take the initiative and find out the name of the hirer.

550. Keep in mind that ten focused resumes addressed to the correct people are worth one hundred mass mailings to "Dear Human Resources Director." You substantially increase the odds that someone will read your resume when you specifiy the recipient. Don't use "Dear Sales Manager" just because it's hard to find the name of the right person. Keep searching. Sending your resume to Sales Manager is no more effective than "To Whom It May Concern."

551.

Take your cue from the employer. If you're responding to an ad, send your resume via the requested method: mail, fax, email, etc.

552. Don't call to question why you should fax your resume when email is the medium of exchange for this millennium. Working has a lot to do with following directions and edicts. If you refuse to follow directions when you're merely looking for a job, the company folks won't believe that you could follow directions if they were to hire you. Frankly, you'll just seem troublesome ("I saw your ad, but I'd rather email my resume, OK?"). Not OK. Instead, show how cooperative you are. Go to a copying store if you don't have a fax machine, and do it the way the hiring manager requested.

553. Respond by mail. You may mail a resume in response to a newspaper ad, Internet ad, or you may even send an unsolicited resume. Whatever prompts you to mail a resume, make sure that you have the correct name of the designated recipient, correct name and spelling of the company, and the right street, suite, city, state, and zip code.

554.
Don't send your resume without the correct zip code, or your resume may end up in the post office lost-and-found. Look up zip codes for addresses in the United States by referring to the U.S. Postal Service website, www.usps.gov. See the tab "Finding a Zip Code."

555. Only conduct a mass-mail campaign with the knowledge that there's no guarantee you will get your resume into the right hands. Sending out hundreds of resumes to target companies and simply hoping that your resume will wind up on the appropriate desk is a long shot. You have to assume that the resume will take the proper route, someone will read it and be entranced, that person will pick up the phone and invite you for a visit, and finally, offer you a job. What are the odds?

556. Heighten your chances of getting an interview from an unsolicited resume by calling to make sure the person received the resume and asking if he would be interested in talking to you. After you send an unsolicited resume by mail, call five working days later. This gives the hiring manager time to receive your resume and not enough time to lose it under other paperwork.

557. Follow faxing etiquette. When ads or job postings ask you to fax a resume, send it that way. (On a formality scale, faxing is somewhere between mail and email.) Send your resume with a fax transmittal form. You can use one of the fax transmittal templates in Microsoft Office or make your own. Make the fax transmittal form professional. Type it if you can. Include the name of the person whom you want to receive the fax, her fax number, as well as your name, fax number, and phone number. That way, if the fax is misplaced, it still gets to the right person. Fax a separate cover letter with your resume to explain why you're perfect for the job. (See chapter 21 on cover letters.)

558.

Email your resume. If the online job posting indicates that you should email your resume and it lists a designated party, it will wind up in the right hands.

559.

Make sure you email your resume professionally. Don't just send it as an attachment with no explanation of why you're sending your resume.

560.

Triple-check the email address to make sure it is correct.

561.

If a want ad is listed as a blind ad, follow instructions and do not track down the company behind the ad. Blind ads are posted that way for a reason. The position might be confidential, and the hiring manager doesn't want employees or outsiders to know the job opening exists, or a company may list a blind ad because the human resources department doesn't want to handle the numerous phone calls that follow job advertisements. Another reason could be that the company has a turnover problem and doesn't want people to know that it's once again trying to fill a position. Be respectful of the preference of a company that places a blind ad. You probably won't get a warm reception if you figure out who's behind it, so don't try to track down the source.

562. When you're responding to a position posted on a job board or company web site, follow one of two methods. For a job posting, there is usually a link to an email address where you attach or cut-and-paste your resume, and include a short, accomplishment–driven email cover letter. It makes sense to both attach and cut-and-paste your resume because some virus protection programs may not let your attachment through. Or you can register with each job board, which takes some time in setting up your information but allows you to respond to subsequent postings with ease.

563. Using a job board is a good way to get your name and resume in front of a company. Job boards do work. But remember that when you see a job posting, so do millions of other people in the world. That doesn't mean they are all as qualified as you, but it does mean they may respond, and the sheer volume can really delay the process. Think of a job board as a long shot. With newspaper employment ads, on the other hand, the audience is usually limited to a specific geographic area, whereas the Internet literally has no geographic boundaries, so the entire world gets to see the job listings.

564. Don't think for one minute that some poor human resources person studies every one of the countless resumes submitted to an Internet job posting. It's much more likely that the job board or company uses a keyword search engine to look for five or so keywords that are important to the position (see more on how this works in chapters 24 and 25).

565. Get your resume in the right hands by anticipating keyword searches; describe your jobs by using special industry words. If you want a nursing job, for example, you use *healthcare delivery, patient care*, etc. Failure to use the right terms may put you too low in the sorting process and so you lose out on some categories that are exactly what you do. Put keywords in your Summary of Experience or Skills Summary, which appears at the beginning of your resume, after your contact information. This summary gives the reader a quick view of your background, experience, and accomplishments, and should feature the best of what you have to offer a prospective employer. Use words that are most recognized in your job title, functional area, and industry.

566.

When you call to follow up on a resume you've sent, stay on message. Sound positive and upbeat. Deliver your message in about thirty seconds and then listen to the response.

567.

When you fax a resume, call within forty-eight hours to make sure that the fax went through. Sometimes faxes don't make it to their destination; other times, they end up in the trash. Another fiasco is when your faxed resume goes to the wrong person.

568.

Make a follow-up call after emailing your resume. Like faxing, email is not without glitches, and often when an email fails to go through, you don't receive an error message. Follow up within twenty-four hours after sending to make sure that your resume found its way safely through cyberspace.

569. Send a follow-up email to a blind ad in twenty-four hours to confirm receipt. Ideally, if there is a name on the email address, you can figure out who the resume-receiver is and call to confirm. You may want to schedule another call in five working days for feedback on your resume. Some hiring managers will consider this a positive sign of "assertiveness," while another may brand you a pest for having called once. Probably better to err on the side of conservatism; don't overdo your follow-up.

570. Remember the caveat for email. Email addresses change faster than physical mail addresses, so double check to make sure that the email address is current. If you're responding to a newspaper ad or job board posting, you can assume that the email address is correct, but if you're sending a resume to an email address from someone's business card, don't assume—ask.

571. If you have business cards from your contacts, email your resume to those addresses after calling to make sure it's OK. You know you're getting these resumes into the hands of people you've met who may have some connections that can help you get a job. But don't send a barrage of resumes to those cards. The person on the other end may not remember you, may no longer be at that email address, or may not care about your job search.

572. Use the company web site to research the correct email address and name spelling of the hiring manager. If you don't find your contact, you can determine the email address protocol for the company and create the address. Send the email address a couple of different ways to ensure that it will arrive. Type your second-best guesses in the blind copy area, bcc.

573. Use search engines like Google or Yahoo to research email addresses. You can also use boards such as Switchboard.

574.

Carry your resume with you everywhere, as another means of getting it in the right hands of people who can help you. Keep copies in 8½ x 11-inch envelopes in your car or briefcase. That way, at every networking opportunity, you have a resume you can hand out. A networking opportunity can be anytime that you're with anyone.

575.

Ask friends for referrals and for delivery. A friend can deliver your resume to the hiring manager or company recruiter either by paper or by forwarding the email resume you send to them. A referral from an existing employee, assuming that person is in good standing in the company, is more powerful that an email coming from you, a stranger.

576.

To get your resume into the right hands, you may have to learn different social etiquette if your culture discourages overly aggressive behavior. Some Europeans aren't used to promoting themselves and working hard to get resumes in the right hands. One man from

Switzerland tells of the difficulty he had in overcoming the training of his culture, where being assertive in presenting resumes to hiring managers is frowned upon.

577. If necessary, drop in. Typically, dropping in on businesspeople doesn't delight them, but if you draw a circle around your house and canvas that area, dropping off resumes and asking for brief interviews, it may work for you to scout around in your nearby geographical area, and in that case, your dropping by won't seem out of the ordinary or overly needy. Or if there is a company you really want to work for, hand carry a resume and politely ask to see a hiring manager (say that you don't have an appointment but will take just a few minutes, and be sure you take no more than five minutes).

578.
Be creative in your efforts to get your resume in the right hands. You may be able to send a small sample of your work that your company doesn't regard as confidential or private, such as a CD. Use this for target companies that interest you the most.

579. Don't submit several copies of your resume to different departments in one company. That practice is frowned upon. Don't alter your resume to emphasize skills in different ways and then send it to one company with customized copies for various departments. Don't do anything sneaky to get your resume in the right hands.

580. To make an impression with the arrival of your resume (because you really want to work at the company), try an unusual method of conveyance. Get the name, title, and address of the hiring manager, and send your resume and cover letter via a local delivery service, Federal Express, UPS, or U.S. Priority Mail. This gets expensive, so use the unique presentation sparingly. Priority Mail, for example, is about 10 times more expensive than a regular first-class stamp, but it's still cheaper than overnight services. On the other hand, Priority Mail has a certain amount of snob appeal, which gives it more impact than a regular piece of mail; try it if a company really excites you.

581. Follow up periodically. One call probably won't be enough to ensure that your resume will get an audience. If you reach the person you sent your resume to and he says, "got it, but haven't read it yet," just ask when you can call back to answer questions. Then call at the time suggested. If you don't reach your recipient, call until you do. You can leave a message, but it's doubtful that you'll get a return call, which is why you may want to call until you talk to the person you're trying to contact. But don't leave messages five times in one day! Even when you don't talk to someone, you're making an impression; the hiring manager will notice the five "please call" slips and chalk you up as desperate or nutty.

582. Show respect for a human resources director by copying her when you send your resume to a specific hiring manager. That way, you're covered in both departments and you don't have to wait for human resources to funnel your resume to the right hiring person.

583.
Keep track of what you've done in the way of spreading yourself around. After you databank your resume in job banks, make note of them so you'll know where you're listed.

584. If you've put your resume into a million hands by sending it to every job site, let your recruiter know what's going on. He may not want to waste time trying to place you when you're hustling all over the Net.

17.

Ensure Response to Your Resume

After your resume has flown on its way, you may wonder whether it has actually reached its destination. It's fine to follow up with a short, polite phone call, but don't bombard the company with daily phone calls: "What did you think of my resume? Do you plan to interview me? What's taking you guys so long?"

Instead, stay calm. Observe these guidelines for the period after the resume has been sent:

585. Phone in. You may get a call for an interview just because you sent a resume, but it's much more likely that the resume you sent is under a stack of 99 others, or in someone's in-box. If you want results, you better follow up.

586. Be assertive, but not obnoxious. No one is conspiring to keep you from getting the job you want, but unless a company is desperate for help, hiring isn't actually a hiring manager's number-one priority. Be persistent, but remember that you're selling and the company is buying. If you're pushy or rude, your resume will get tossed.

587.
Make sure you pursue the right person. If you call and call, only to find out that the person you're calling has nothing to do with hiring, ask the receptionist for the name of the hiring manager.

588. When you catch up with the hirer, make sure you have your story straight. Say who you are and why you're calling: "Jane, this is Sally Christopher. I sent you a resume by mail about a week ago for the Senior Chemical Engineer position, and I wanted to see if you got it. Is this a good time to call?" Jane will probably say no and no—she doesn't remember receiving it (lost, stolen, forgotten, ignored), and she's busy (everyone is). Then, your response is: "All right, I'll send another resume. How should I send it?" Jane may say to email it. Unless she has said she's busy, get the correct spelling of the email address, ask if you can call again in three days, and quickly mention two things that make you especially well qualified for the job. Don't overuse the person's name as if she's your new friend. False familiarity breeds contempt. The hiring manager doesn't know you and won't want to if you're presumptuous or pushy.

589.

When you get a hiring person on the phone, your talk should be brief and action-oriented. Make sure that what you say lasts no longer than thirty seconds. You make more progress by listening than talking.

590. Know what not to say. When you're leaving a voice mail message for an employment agency, here's the kind of thing you shouldn't say: "Hey there, I'm Suzy Mess, a twenty-nine-year-old mom with four kids. I really want to be a photo stylist even though I don't know exactly what a photo stylist does. I like to be around celebrities because I have lots of talent myself, and it gives me a chance to tell them about it, just in case they want to discover someone. I always had to work at stupid jobs with mean bosses. That was a bummer, but now I'm moving on, and I hope you'll take a chance on me because I have good people skills even though my last boss said I sucked at working with people. I'm dying to work around celebs and other important people. I read every gossip column I can find and *Teen People*. And here's what else you need to know about me...." Enough already! In other words, if you don't know how to leave a message that sounds professional, don't leave one at all.

591. Schedule subsequent follow-ups based on the company rep's recommendation.

592. Don't nag or pester. If someone tells you not to call again because it won't help your chances, believe it. On the other hand, if no one stops you from calling, follow your own judgment and check on the status of your resume every week or two. But be aware that anything resembling nagging definitely hurts your chances. And never make the mistake of thinking that the receptionist lacks clout. In some companies, the receptionist tells the powers-that-be which job candidates are obnoxious and not worth pursuing because they were trouble on the telephone.

593. Cultivate rapport with the receptionist of the company you're courting. The phone-answerer can be your ally. Conversely, if you're nasty, the receptionist may flex his or her power muscles and decide not to put your calls through. Early on, ask the receptionist's name and call him by it, but don't overdo the "Hey, Hal, good to talk to you." And don't engage a receptionist in long chats when you know he needs to cover the phones and probably handles the front desk, too.

594. Don't sound desperate (even if you are). When you speak to a company representative, business acquaintance, or social contact, stay optimistic and cheerful. Even if you have been out of work for two years and your furniture is being repossessed as you speak, summon up a perky, professional tone. Don't say, "For god's sake, I'll do anything—I'll take any job you have." Stick to your positive script and get the job you want. Desperation doesn't net jobs.

595. Don't whine. Hiring managers want bright, happy, energetic people who will add value to the bottom line. Don't make a call unless you're sure that you can act upbeat. Sometimes, just smiling as you talk on the phone makes your voice sound animated.

596. Don't take out your frustrations on the receptionist or hiring manager. If you've worked at one company for a long time, you may hate dealing with the rejection that can come with a job search. You may experience extreme frustration if you've been working high on the corporate ladder and now face fewer job choices. The same goes for people in fields with limited job openings. One magazine editor tells of feeling the crunch when a magazine she worked for folded and she found only one job in her field in the entire metropolitan area of Chicago. (That means it's time to figure out how your skills carry over to another type of work.)

Whatever your situation, it won't help your cause to take out your frustration on a company rep. Instead, be respectful to all concerned. The old saying "what goes around, comes around" is absolutely true. (See chapter 22 for ways to lighten up while you wait for your resume to net interviews.)

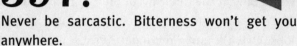

597.
Never be sarcastic. Bitterness won't get you anywhere.

598.
Don't issue a deadline. Remember who's buying and who's selling. You can ask about the hiring manager's timeframe, but it's not smart to give an ultimatum: "I need to know whether you're going to hire me by this Friday—do you hear me?" If you have another job offer, it's all right to say that a second company needs a response by X date. But be sure to convey this information casually and bear in mind that the hiring manager you're talking to doesn't necessarily care if you have another offer deadline.

599. Follow up with friends. Just because you gave your resume to a friend of yours to pass on to a company rep, don't assume that the resume got there. Politely follow up within five working days of having handed or emailed your resume. Say: "Just wanted to check to see if you've had time to get my resume into the right hands...."

600. Circle back to friends you gave resumes even if they had no job leads. Stay at the forefront of their minds. And, for those friends who are pushing your resume at their jobs, give a friendly reminder: "Please don't forget your buddy who's jobless."

601.

Follow up on resumes you gave to acquaintances at soccer games, art openings, and the zoo. Check back with new contacts in four or five days and then again a month later.

602. Keep tabs on resumes you have sent out that are associated with business networking. You may accumulate a mountain of business cards in the course of your networking and job-search activities so keep these organized; mark on each card if you sent a resume to that contact to pass on—or if the person hinted that he may arrange an interview. Wait five days and then phone each person you gave or sent a resume; if nothing happens, follow up again in a month.

603. Keep your game face on. Hiring managers and human resources reps get many calls, most of which they view as interruptions. You may notice that the only people who return your phone calls promptly are salespeople. Follow their example and return calls promptly; develop the ability to sound happy when you receive or originate a call. People like to talk to perky people because it cheers them up.

604. Don't talk their heads off. Say who you are, why you're calling, and what you want. Don't be evasive because you think it's indelicate to ask for what you want. Be direct.

605. When you make a call, if you aren't sure what you want, describe your dilemma and ask for guidance. Most people are flattered when you ask them for help.

606. Ask for referrals within a company. Most companies have multiple hiring managers and multiple ways to get inside. One hiring manager may know of a need in another department. Don't be shy; ask, "Is there anyone else in the company whom I should talk to?"

607.

If you fail to reach the person you're trying to contact (he or she's never at his or her desk and you've left messages that weren't returned), try a fax. Some people don't return phone calls, but do respond to the written word.

608. Turn to email when you finally reach rolling-boil frustration. You've left messages, called at odd times (before 8 AM, at lunch, after 5 PM). Many busy supervisors respond to emails even though they ignore other types of communication. They like that they can read email at their convenience and respond with a click (and *without* a big conversation).

609. Mix it up. Communicate with human resources representatives via phone, fax, and email. See what works. Most people have a preferred form of communication; you just have to figure out what it is. Ask the receptionist, "What's the best way to contact Ms. Slippery Slope? Does she prefer email?"

610. Schedule a second communication via fax. If you leave a few messages that get no response, a fax may motivate a company representative to action.

611.
Schedule a second communication via email. After you've left a phone message or two, follow up by email.

612. Drop by. If the company you're interested in is close, consider hand delivering a resume. Ask if you can speak to someone in the Z department, or ask for someone in human resources.

613. Set a schedule for follow-up. Most hiring managers are too busy to respond to your first, second, or even third call. A rule of thumb in sales is that it takes seven contacts to make a sale, so it's quite possible that it may take seven contacts for you to get an interview. Each call, fax, and email counts.

614. Understand that there's no guarantee anyone will read your resume. But you can follow up diligently and work the numbers.

615. Expect a positive response to a resume to come in about one to three weeks if you responded to an Internet posting or a newspaper ad. If you don't hear anything, that doesn't automatically mean you got passed over, but the chances are slimmer. However, some companies take months to get back to people—there's no set rule on response time.

616.

Keep in mind that companies are swamped with resumes, which means no news could be good news.

617.

Don't be surprised if you respond to an Internet posting and receive a computer-generated acknowledgment saying "Thanks for submitting and we'll file your resume in cyberspace and call you later"—or you'll hear nothing, ever.

618.

Don't take rejection personally. You're not qualified for every job, and every job is not for you. Plus, job descriptions contain only the bare-bones requirements to attract resumes, while in the background sits a whole set of preferred requirements that weed out most resumes submitted.

619. While you're navigating the circuitous waters of the job search, you will talk to some people you'll like and others you won't, but always summon up your professional best and be respectful all-around. You never know whom you may run across in another workplace. If a receptionist or hiring manager treats you unkindly, just assume he's having a bad day and cut him some slack.

620. Look at the job and company from the hiring manager's point of view. In the process of the job search, practice empathy. Ask yourself, "Whom would I hire for this position? What qualities would I look for if I were hiring for this position?" Consider how well your background and skills match. You will probably gain points by adopting this viewpoint when you talk to hiring managers.

621. Don't obsess about one job. You may become smitten by a certain job listing. You decide that this is the one for you before you even have an interview. You research the company, read the job posting over and over, and imagine yourself doing the job, sitting in the office, spending the money. This is a futile preoccupation. It's fine to get excited about job opportunities, but don't turn any position into a fantasy.

622.

Don't stop looking, calling, faxing, and emailing just because you had a good interview. Stop looking the day you accept a new job. And even after that, stay connected to your network so that if you ever need assistance again, you'll have it.

623. Understand that you may get a "no" quickly, or you may never hear a word about the resume you submitted.

18.

Know the Pet Peeves of Hiring Managers and Headhunters

Recruiters and hiring managers develop resume pet peeves because their lives revolve around dealing with these often-misunderstood communications. For every resume oddity, there's a story. Read on—and don't make these mistakes!

624. Avoid being too good to be true. One recruiter recalls a candidate who had not just good grades but great grades. She had listed on her resume that she had a 4.0 from the University of Honolulu. The recruiter decided to check out her GPA, and found that she didn't have a 4.0 and there was no University of Honolulu. (A real 4.0 student could at least have manufactured a story with a real university!)

625. Don't try to trick your headhunter. One recruiter tells of a job candidate who listed a degree from the University of Houston, but when the recruiter called to verify the degree, there was no record of that person. When contacted, the candidate claimed, "Oh, I graduated from another branch, the downtown branch." No record. Upon next contact, the candidate produced a letter that documented the degree on University of Houston letterhead. But the recruiter spotted a fake because "college" was misspelled.

626. Watch out for dateless wonders. Recruiters see many resumes that list a candidate's university and a major, but no dates of attendance. They assume that the job candidate graduated ages ago and wants to conceal his old age, or that this person never graduated. If you're an oldster who tries this technique, you must be ready to produce your correct date for a background check. If you didn't list dates because your degree is fictional, reconsider being a fraud. Why not be who you really are?

627. Know the power of the rumor mill. One recruiter recalls a woman who claimed she had a degree from a school in Birmingham, Alabama. "I used to live there," she said. But the school's name didn't ring a bell, and investigation revealed that it was a mail-order mill. The moral of the story: If you got a degree from a mail-order house, warn your recruiter so that he can handle explaining that to a potential employer.

628.

Don't lie on applications or resumes because recruiters and hiring managers hate fabrications more than anything. You'll be history once they find out and decide you're nothing but trouble.

629. Plan well. One headhunter tells of a man whose good resume got him a job, after which the company scheduled a drug test. Having partied on the weekend, he failed the drug test, which cost him the job.

630. Use the right word at the right time. When you write a resume, be careful of soundalike words (their/there). You can spell them right and not detect any error on spell checking, but you've still used the wrong word and your otherwise flawless resume is tarnished. Write carefully, proof carefully, and ask a friend to proof. Let your resume sit for twenty-four hours after you have written it. When you pick it up again, you can review it with fresh eyes and spot errors.

631.

Eliminate extracurricular activities that speak to religion, political persuasion, or sexual persuasion.

632. Do list activities that attest to your expertise. If you're a writer, the International Association of Business Communicators is a plus. If you are a CPA, belonging to a state organization such as the California Society of CPAs works in your favor. If you were on the Stanford University golf team and consistently shot under par, an interviewer may be intrigued. Kevin Wakeem, a tax accountant at a large energy company, got an interview because he had been a ski instructor in Colorado. That information caught the eye of an interviewer, and Wakeem got a job as a property tax accountant. The interviewer decided that Wakeem's outgoing communication skills (as a ski instructor) worked well with the negotiation skills needed for negotiating property tax values.

Alex Oey, a former championship weightlifter in college, put that background on his resume, and it helped him get an interview for a job as an engineer. The hiring manager was impressed, viewing his athletic record as an indication of drive and energy.

633. Avoid negatives. Hiring managers and recruiters hate negativity. Selling yourself and your experience in person and on paper is all about being positive. If your department was eliminated due to financial difficulties, don't say "Due to financial mismanagement, department was eliminated." While that may be true, saying so makes you look disloyal. Instead, say that the job was eliminated because the department was eliminated.

634. To keep from confusing head-hunters and hiring managers, use the right verb tense. If you're currently at a certain company, present your work in present tense. Example: "Assist students in admissions, registration, course advising, course transferability, and financial aid." When you're referring to a past job, use past tense. Say: "Solved infestation and maintenance problems and responded to resident complaints in a timely manner. Supervised groundskeepers and housekeeping personnel."

635.
Expect a tongue-lashing from headhunters if your resume has misspellings. Your resume reflects your skills and experience and also your attention to detail and desire to produce a quality product. Your resume is your "product." Make spell-check your friend.

636. Don't appear to be out of the loop. Hiring managers hate it when they know more about company changes (in your past jobs) than you do. Has your prior employer been bought and sold numerous times? Stay abreast of changes and reflect them on your resume. If you worked for First National Bank of Nantucket, which is now called Bank of America, write that down. Your resume looks outdated if you fail to use the company's current name. To be 100 percent correct, list the current name of the company as well as its name when you worked there: Bank of America (formerly known as First National Bank of Nantucket) 1990–1992.

637.

Don't use clichés. Headhunters are sick of them; hiring managers' eyes glaze over. Some of the clichés they don't want to see are: willing to do whatever it takes; the hardest worker you've ever met; fit as a fiddle; healthy as a horse; hard as nails; tough as a bear. Don't waste precious words on puff stuff.

638. Avoid overused industry phrases. At the top of the list in the human resources hall of fame are the worn-out terms "entry level, self-starter, hard worker, positive attitude, team player." These are pointless. Entry level is someone who has just graduated from high school or university and is looking for a job, and something that obvious doesn't bear repeating. The other descriptions are so subjective that you're smarter to show that you're a "hard worker" or "self-starter" by listing accomplishments that prove that fact.

639. Don't be nonsensical. The person who reads your resume—hiring manager, human resources professional, or recruiter—gives the words a thirty-second once-over, looking for a quick take on what you're all about. This is a rapid process, and if the reader fails to get a feel for you in a matter of seconds, your resume won't proceed to the next step.

640.
Beware of overkill! You can have too many buzz-words. Don't try to dazzle resume readers with technical terms to show how brilliant you are. Instead, communicate skills and experience in a clear and common sense way.

641. Avoid being too generic. Just like recruiters and hiring managers don't want you to baffle them with techno-speak, don't make your resume so politically correct and bland that no one can figure out what you're talking about. Vague won't help your case. You don't want your resume to look like it came from a template in a book or was lifted from sentences in a job description. Give specifics.

642. Don't make your resume so technical that a reader has no idea what you've done. This is the flip side of making your resume too generic. If your resume is highly technical and specific, it may take an equally skilled and educated reader to decipher it—and what if there's no one like that in the human resources department? You can prepare a technical version of your resume for the person you will report to, but expect your resume to first pass through the hands of recruiters, human resources professionals, and many others, who may fail to get the drift of what you've done and fail to pass on your resume to the department manager who can offer you the job.

643. Fix unintelligible titles. Large corporations sometimes give titles that bear little or no resemblance to the real world. Use these and hiring managers, human resources professionals, and recruiters won't know what you did. Resumes are outlines of your experience. If integral parts, such as titles, don't make sense, this may cause someone to bypass your resume for one that's more easily understood. For example, if you had the title "Staff B," who knows what you did for that company? Staff B may speak volumes internally, but those aren't the folks you need to impress. The answer? Modify the title to fit what you really did—call it "Staff Auditor" on your resume.

644. Remember that your references may not recognize a title you substituted for clarity. Example: The last place you worked, you were "Assistant," but for resume purposes, you changed this to "Secretary to CEO and Board Members." If the company wants to verify references and asks for a list, explain that you "translated" your title to make it communicate better what you actually did on that job. Wait, however, until someone asks for references.

645. Don't enrage headhunters by using a type size that looks like legal fine print. "More than once, we have seen candidates dump absolutely everything onto their resume, from birth to the present time," says one recruiter. "And to make it fit on one or two pieces of paper, they use eight-point type. This is hard to read, and some hiring managers' eyes don't work well enough to read such small print."

646.
Don't anesthetize recruiters and hiring managers with huge blocks of gray text with no white space. Your resume shouldn't look like a page out of a book or magazine.

647. Remember that recruiters and hiring managers despise really long resumes. A multi-page resume suggests a lack of awareness of the business world. The exception is a medical, academic, or government curriculum vitae (CV), which can be longer.

648. Understand that savvy hiring managers will notice if you use a functional resume to hide a dicey work history. Human resources professionals, hiring managers, and recruiters dislike functional resumes because they see them as attempts to hide job-hopping or jail time. So, unless you have a long list of employers, a stint in jail, or you're trying to make a career change, stick with reverse chronological.

649. You can be sure that headhunters spot a padded resume every time. Fluffing up your resume to get a job that you're not qualified for isn't smart. "We have heard of a few candidates in the many years we have been in the search business that pumped up their work experience to get a much better job than their background allowed, and they lasted about a month," says one longtime recruiter. "Don't do this to yourself. Play it straight and don't fluff up your resume."

650. Avoid the dateless resume or the one with overlapping dates. One recruiter dislikes resumes without dates because he doesn't want to have to guess when the applicant worked at which place. Least favorite of recruiters and hiring managers is a functional resume with no dates (it's impossible to tell when the applicant did what and where). With the time involved in looking at the volume of resumes floated to companies these days, hiring managers don't want to puzzle out your resume.

651. End up Most Hated Job Candidate if you email a resume with a virus. Be a good cyberspace citizen and install an antivirus software package on your computer—Norton Antivirus, for example. An antivirus package is inexpensive and can save you a world of trouble, in both receiving and sending attachments over the Internet. Sending or receiving a virus is bad for your job-search business and the recipient's business. Also, remember to update your antivirus package weekly. Also consider getting a firewall to keep your e-resumes safe. A firewall is a set of related programs that protects a private network or individual computer from users associated with other networks. A firewall looks at each document or email and decides whether to let the document into your system. Look at F-Secure or Zone Alarm, from Zone Labs.

652.

Always remember to take along your resume when you interview. Hiring managers, recruiters, and human resources professionals may get irritated when you forget to bring your resume to an interview. It slows everyone down. And, having to fill out an application without your resume in hand will definitely test your memory. Also, not having your resume when you answer questions about prior employers can try an interviewer's patience. The answer is simple: Take your resume to every interview, whether you think that the interviewer already has a copy or not.

653. Recruiters emphasize following the rules for applying. In the era of online activities, you can complete some applications from the comfort of your personal computer, but many companies want you to come in to fill out an application on-site. They may want to see how long it takes you to fill out the application, how neatly and completely you do it, how interested you seem, and whether you can follow directions. In some cases, an in-person application is just standard operating procedure; in another instance, the company may use a handwriting analyst to assess candidates. But no matter what the company's motivation, fill out the application according to instructions. Do keep in mind that the legal lingo at the end means that you must tell the truth; signing your name on the form means you're verifying the truthfulness of what you put on the application. Immediate dismissal can occur if falsifications come to light.

19.

Fielding Problems That Arise Regarding Resumes

If you've searched other chapters looking for an answer to your special situation, check out the following resume issues and tips on how to handle them:

654. A company representative called but you could tell that he hadn't read your resume, so what's the proper response? Well, don't say "What's wrong with you? I can tell you haven't looked at my resume!" Instead, answer his questions.

655.

You called a hiring manager but never got a response? Call and don't leave a message, or leave a message every other day. Leave no more than three messages when you haven't heard anything at all. More than that could be considered stalking.

656.

Every time you follow up on a resume, a company rep swears he never got it? Human resources people are bombarded with resumes, phone calls, and other types of input. When someone does a phone follow-up, it's common to hear that no one remembers receiving your resume. This may mean the company didn't get it, someone lost it, or it has already been thrown it in the trash. Just offer to send another copy of your resume, do so, and follow up after that.

657. Worried what the hiring manager will think about all the temp work on your resume? Be ready to explain. Maybe you were laid off, or maybe you just preferred to work temp. Either way, it's a good idea to talk about that big stretch of temp work correctly, and don't try to make it look like a full-time job. Clearly present the dates you did temp work and list skills and experience gained. Make lemonade out of this potential lemon. Temp work gives you a variety of functional skills and exposure to different industries; you can capitalize on that variety.

658. You can present years of temp experience on your resume without letting it become twelve pages long. You can give each temp assignment as many bullet points as a full time job, but if you have a new temp assignment every month, you may have a very long resume. Better, just hit the highlights—include temp assignments that provided the best experience and the best ratings. Talk about the assignments where you excelled.

659.

Wondering what to say on your resume about the time you were fired? Don't mention this on a resume. If an interviewer nails you ("I heard you were fired from your last job—is that true?"), be honest. But don't place blame. Just be factual.

660.

Confused about how to handle temp jobs that turned into full-time ones? When you worked temp first and then the company hired you full time, don't surrender to the temptation to extend your tenure on your resume. Separate the time you worked temp and the time you worked full time.

661.

You've had a succession of similar jobs at lots of different places? Finesse these job changes on your resume so that it looks like your career has some continuity. Try grouping positions.

662. Worried about how to frame a company buyout? If the firm has had several names in five years because it has been sold three times, here's how you handle this situation on your resume:

First National Bank of Lincoln, Lincoln, Nebraska 1997–present

(Formerly known as Lincoln First Savings Bank, Lincoln Savings Institution, Nebraska Savings)

663. Eight jobs in five years? Let's presume you're restless. Write a resume that doesn't draw attention to the fact that you've had eight jobs in five years. If you've worked in a similar job or function, group your jobs together. If you've changed jobs frequently, include the reasons for changes with short, factual explanations (no insulting employers).

664.

Work-history gaps are in the past five years? Insert a sentence of explanation after the last job before the gap.

665. Worried about your interview skills? Learn how to interview like a champ so you'll be ready when your resume reaps interviews. (See chapter 28 for tips on interviewing.) Ask about the position, the department, and the company and show the company representative that you make sense for all three. Use your resume as a guide to help you explain your strengths as benefits to the company.

666. Fearful that a past employer may give a poor reference? Don't be afraid to ask a boss from your past what he will say if contacted about you as a former employee—and listen carefully to the answer. If you ask a one-time supervisor what he plans to say about you and he dodges the question, ask a friend to call as a pseudo-hirer and check. Provide sample questions to make the covert checkup easy:

- What were the exact dates of the candidate's employment with your firm?
- What was the candidate's title/position?
- What was his/her parting compensation?
- What were his/her primary responsibilities?
- Based on your knowledge, why did the candidate leave your firm?
- What was the candidate's record of attendance?
- How would you describe the candidate's work habits?

667. Disappointed that no one wants to see your portfolio? If your field is photography, design, architecture, advertising, journalism, or public relations, you may be itching to show someone what's in your portfolio. Perhaps you even have an online portfolio in addition to the one you physically cart around. Unfortunately, fewer employers are willing to look at portfolios. Graphic art is an exception—you definitely won't get hired until your portfolio charms someone at the company. If you do find a hiring manager who will check out your portfolio, she may ask you to leave it so that other staffers can peruse it too, which means you need an extra one. It's always possible you'll never see it again.

668.
Preparing a new resume because a takeover is coming? Your firm is a takeover candidate, and the main pursuer is known for axing employees to make the bottom line look better. Then you should pull out your old resume as a guide and get busy. Take old evaluations, job descriptions, and sketch out the basics: company, location, dates, and fill in accomplishments, duties, and responsibilities.

669. Want to hide the fact that you've never had a job you liked? Write a resume that camouflages your work malaise. List duties you performed. Think of things you accomplished during your time working and focus on those things—what you did to help save time, save money, or make money, for various companies.

670. Want to write an accomplishment-driven resume? If your goal is a good-paying job with opportunity for growth, you must show a potential employer how you can add value and make his life better with you on his staff. An accomplishment-driven resume is one that cites outstanding things you've done and makes them the focus of the resume.

671.

Wonder if your statements are weighty enough? Of the following two, which is more likely to net an interview? "Performed accounts receivable aging." Or: "Increased cash flow from accounts receivable by 20 percent, or $120,000 weekly, via review, analysis, and timely communication of outstanding accounts receivable." Enough said.

672. Worried about your boss discovering your job search? About 99 percent of the time, no one really cares who's sending out resumes—until a company decides to interview the candidate. Sheer volume and overload are your friends. But many fields of specialty are small worlds and people do talk. So, if you can't risk your employer finding out that you are looking, don't float your resume. Do, however, conduct a campaign of networking and word of mouth. (See confidentiality tips in chapter 20.) Don't use your work Internet access to send resumes; many companies review the emails sent in and sent out of their systems (it's their property, and they have the right to look at any email sent or received on the company system). Find other places to send your resume via email. Most public libraries and some coffee houses offer Internet access, or find a friend who will let you go online at his home.

673. What should you say about an employer that folded in disgrace? If this is your most recent employer, you can refer to "a large independent energy company," but if you live in a place like Houston, people will know that you're talking about Exxon. However, if you worked for a subsidiary with a different name, you can use that. Most importantly, when you describe your skills and experience, make it clear that you didn't work in the departments that brought down the company.

If it's a firm you worked for many years ago, defend the experience without championing the company. Never criticize a former employer; a hiring manager will simply imagine his company as the future object of your ridicule.

674. Wondering how to handle jobs in several different industries? Because this kind of resume can be very confusing, use a functional resume. Divide your skills and experience into the various industries or according to functional areas. Make it as simple as possible for the reader to understand your background.

675. Should you disclose that rehab stint? Your resume markets you, your skills, your work ethic, and what you bring to the table. You don't have to explain a drug or alcohol problem in your past unless it's the reason behind huge gaps in your job history. If so, you can attribute the gaps to "an illness that is no longer an issue," or say that you took time off. Other data that are equally inappropriate for a resume are: homelessness, fights with coworkers and bosses, firings, chronic illnesses, credit problems, common-law marriages, same-sex living arrangements, illegitimate children, lawsuits.

676. Concerned that some employers can act suspicious of self-employment? If you have had your own business for five-plus years or have been self-employed for five or more years, employers may be skeptical of your background and qualifications. Sometimes, they unfairly discount work that you've done on your own when, in truth, owning a small business or working as a contract employee teaches a multitude of skills. You learn the product or service, as well as finance, accounting, operations, management, leasing, and other entrepreneurial skills. Nevertheless, you, as a former businessperson or self-employed person, must meet the challenge of communicating your special experience to potential employers by including quantifiable achievements, not just a laundry list of responsibilities.

677.

Worried about that year you spent traveling? There was a time when taking off two years for world travel would be a career–limiting move, but today, that's not necessarily the case. Most employers have a global view; they realize that every job is temporary and that life is short and should be experienced. During an interview, you can tell the company representative your reason for taking a sabbatical. For example, you were laid off with a big severance package, which gave you the money and the time to travel. On your resume, describe what you gained from your world tour; list "heightened level of cultural sensitivity" and "increased fluency in French" as new job skills acquired.

678. Want to know how to handle a change of heart? Let's say you sent a resume to a company, and you didn't hear anything so you accepted another offer. Two weeks later, you get a call from the first company with a job offer. If you desperately want the first job, you can look at its offer, decide which job is better for you, and move forward as soon as possible. Be honest with the company you accepted a job from—and express your deepest apologies. You may even want to add that you hope the door will still be open in the future if your decision doesn't prove to be the right one.

679. Job-hunting for an upcoming geographical move? Changing jobs is difficult enough; changing cities is even more difficult. Companies first look at local candidates who are qualified. Furthermore, hiring managers want to know that you have a good reason for moving. For example, if you're in oil-and-gas, it makes sense to move to Texas. If you have parents in Seattle, moving there wouldn't be out of the ordinary. But if you have no real reason for moving, a human resources director may wonder if you're on a "Wanted" poster somewhere and you're making a run for it. The reasons that don't play well with hiring managers are emotional ones: "Want a change of scenery. Hope to improve my attitude. Looking for a lifetime companion."

680.

Want to modify your resume to find a job over-seas? Add items that make your experience look international. If you've had international intern-ships, international jobs or projects, or have worked or traveled overseas, put that on your resume. If you speak or read a foreign language, list that ability. If you don't have any of these things in your repertoire, put the emphasis on your flexibility, sense of adventure, and readiness to adapt to a new working environment and con-tribute to the bottom line.

681.

Worried about how to list your now-defunct university? During your interview, you can explain that the school you attended went out of business, but don't put the news on your resume. No need to act defensive or make derogatory comments—just deal with the problem head on and mention what you learned while attending that school.

682. Want to play the race card? Although it may not be politically correct to advocate, you can sometimes use minority status to your advantage. Some companies aggressively recruit minority candidates for certain corporate positions. Because many corporations want diversity in their ranks, you may want to list activities that reveal your ethnicity (president of Hispanic Student Union) when you apply for a job with a large corporation.

20.

Proceed with Caution If Your Job Hunt Is a Secret

Since most people look for jobs while employed, most job searches are confidential. But you can take steps to keep your job search under wraps. Sometimes, the fact that your job search is a secret slips the mind of a busy hiring manager's life. He could be in a hurry to fill a position and may forget that calling you will put your current job at risk unless you spell it out clearly. Here are some ways to stay quiet about job-hunting efforts:

683. Don't feel compelled to inform your employer of your job search. Everyone knows it's unwise to quit one job until you have found another.

684.

Don't tell anyone at work about your job hunt— but do get your resume out there.

685. Don't worry constantly about your supervisor discovering that you are looking for a job; supervisors know that most employees are going to look out for themselves. Few companies will fire you just because you are looking—that is, unless your supervisor is planning to get rid of you anyway; in that case, discovering your job search just gives him a good reason to go ahead and fire you.

686. When you send out a resume, ask for confidentiality in your cover letter. Start with a request for confidentiality, and finish up with one more reminder. The reason you want to reiterate your preference for privacy is that the people who read resumes are very busy and thus may need a gentle reminder.

687. On your resume, indicate that your current employer should be considered confidential. If you don't want a human resources person to contact your current employer, put the word "confidential" by that job. Most prospective employers know that they shouldn't contact an employer if you're still working there, but don't take anything for granted. Indicate that the search is confidential and that you don't want your current employer contacted by setting it apart like this: Randall Atkinson Corp, Saucelito, CA (confidential) 2001–present.

688. Ensure confidentiality by changing your name. If you don't want your current employer to know you're looking for a job or you don't want a potential employer to recognize your name, change it just for your resume. Use a nickname (but nothing goofy like Freckles or Wolfman), your middle name, your maiden name, or your wife's maiden name. If you get an interview, immediately explain to the interviewer that your job search is so sensitive that you had to go to great lengths (changing your name) in order to keep it quiet.

689. Ensure privacy by sending your resume "blind." This means leaving your name off the resume altogether. On most Internet job boards, you can post a resume without posting your name, so why not use the same technique for sending highly confidential resumes? Omit your name and address, and include only a contact email or cell-phone number. Don't use an email address that has your name in it; simply get a separate email address to use in your confidential job search from one of the free email services, such as Hotmail.

690.

Leave the name of your current employer off your resume. To make sure that a potential employer doesn't contact your current employer, omit that company from your resume entirely. Instead, describe the industry, size, etc.: Big Four Public Accounting Firm, Major Energy Company, Regional Magazine, Large Modeling Agency, Small Manufacturer of Pins, or Branch of Major Bank Holding Company.

691. Use your home contact numbers: phone, email, or voice mail. You can't use your work number if you're trying to keep your job search confidential. Imagine how embarrassed you would feel if you were on the phone with a hiring manager when suddenly your boss or a nosy colleague walked by and overheard your conversation.

692.

Make job-search-related calls in the morning before you go to work or after work. Check in with a job-search contact by using your cell phone when you are on a break or at lunch. The best way to keep your job search confidential is to do job-search activities outside of your workplace.

693. Keep in mind that even if you have an email address that's separate from your work address, if you access home email from work and send from your home email address, the company server records this activity, which opens you up to scrutiny. Remember that your company owns the server and has the right to monitor emails going back and forth. Nothing is private that is sent to or from your work server.

694. If you don't have access to the Internet at home, use alternate methods to get on the information highway so that you can avoid using work email for a job search. Most public libraries and coffee shops have Internet access, or you can use a friend's Internet connection.

695. Don't use office time to pursue a new job. It's not ethical to search for a job during the time that your company is paying you to work. Instead, use your lunch hour to return calls. Or you can give your current company back the time you spent on your job search by keeping track of it and making sure you put in the time. If you have to make calls during company time, block them together—first thing in the morning, lunchtime, or late afternoon. That way, you can do more of your work without stopping to job hunt.

696. Don't divulge your job hunt until you're in a secure zone. Wait until you have accepted a job offer, and then let your current employer in on the secret of your job search by giving him a businesslike notice that you will be leaving on X date. Give at least two weeks' notice, and more if possible, especially if you have a job of major responsibility that makes it hard to find a suitable replacement.

697. Network confidentially and get your resume circulating. Although confidential networking sounds like a contradiction in terms, the truth is, networking doesn't necessarily mean putting up a hot-air balloon that displays your name and phone number. You can network discreetly. Attend networking functions that provide opportunities to meet people who work for your target companies. Instead of handing out your resume to everyone you meet, get business cards and call those people later to say that you enjoyed meeting them and that you're conducting a confidential job search and want to email a resume.

698.
Remind your references that your job search is a secret.

699. When in doubt, don't mention references when you're distributing resumes. If you don't think you can trust anyone, don't hand over a list of references during the interview process. Tell the company rep that your search is top secret and that you simply can't give out references before an offer is extended. Add that you'll be happy to provide excellent references after the hiring manager makes you a job offer and you have accepted. Offer the reassurance that you understand that any offer is contingent upon successful follow-up (checking references).

700.
Keep in mind that there's a very limited downside to discovery of your job search. However, if your employer has no sense of humor and decides to fire you when she discovers that you're looking for another job, getting the boot will just provide extra incentive to hurry up and find something better.

701. Prepare your resignation letter if you think a job offer is coming, but do this at home (not at work where someone may be looking over your shoulder). When you get an offer, you can accept it and set a start date and then prepare to resign. Write a letter that gives the bare facts: you're leaving, you plan to have your work in order, and your last day will be two to three weeks from the date of notice. Make an appointment with your supervisor and announce your intentions politely and quickly. Basically, repeat what you have said in the letter; don't give a long explanation. The longer you talk, the more likely you are to say something you don't mean to say and give the supervisor something to use against you. Resist the temptation to slip a good-bye-I'm-leaving letter under a supervisor's door. Meet face to face. Even if you hate the place and can't wait to flee, be courteous. The old don't-burn-bridges anthem rings true for many people who need references later or want to return to companies where they have worked previously.

702. Be ready for the possibility of a counter offer when your great resume and confidential job search pay off, and you march into your supervisor's office to say you're quitting. Your boss may say: "Good luck to you on your new job" or "What will it take for you to stay?" or "If we give you a 10 percent raise, will you stay?" If you get a counter offer, you may want to consider why it took your resignation to get this raise. Perhaps a big project is looming, and your boss wants you to stay just to get that out the door? Statistics show that after six months, 90 percent of employees who accept counter offers are no longer employed by the original companies. They leave on their own or the company helps them leave. So be careful if you decide to take a counter offer because, typically, this is just a short-term fix for both sides.

703.

Work hard even though you've already resigned. That annoying one-foot-out-the-door syndrome won't get you a good reference. After giving two weeks' notice, you may feel like a school kid in the final days of the year; what's on your mind is some vacation time. But it's important not to leave loose ends; your boss and colleagues will remember you as much for the way you finished your job as the way you began it. Leave them smiling. You never know when you may want to go back. Numerous employees do backtrack, but employers don't rehire people whose parting ways are tacky or rude.

704. Prepare yourself for the possibility that your boss may get wind of a resume you floated. Of course, you can always deny it and blame the source for poaching your resume, and this may even work. But use that as a last resort because it wrongly casts blame on an innocent party. Better to admit it and say yes, you were approached about a job and curiosity made you look into it. This is only a small fib if you sent your resume in response to an ad; if the ad hadn't enticed you, you wouldn't have submitted your resume, right?

705. Feel confident that most recruiters who have your resume can maintain confidentiality. Naturally, you take a chance every time you send a resume to anyone: employer, friend, networking acquaintance, or recruiter. But numbers and preoccupation are on your side; most people are too busy to talk about you and your job search. Recruiters make their money by helping people find jobs, not jeopardizing careers (they wouldn't be in business very long if they advertised clients' names). However, when you send out resumes to recruiters, do make a point of telling them that your job search is confidential.

706.

Remember that sending your resume to a blind ad constitutes a big risk. Your company may be the one advertising for the job! If you apply for a job listed in a blind ad, use a blind resume; remove your name and use a cell-phone number and an anonymous email address.

707.

When you respond to job postings on company web sites, you have the name of the company, but it's OK to keep your name confidential on your resume. Email to the address the company has listed, and find the name of someone you can call within five days of sending the resume.

708.

Lace job-hunt conversations with mentions of how "private" your job search is. You can use social gatherings to spread the word that you're looking for a job and pick up ideas, and you can hand (or email) someone a copy of your confidential resume and ask that person to pass it on to a potential lead. Ask if he prefers an e-resume, which is easy to forward. Underscore the confidentiality of the mission and emphasize that you put limited contact information in the resume to keep your actions under wraps.

709.

Create a job-search business card to keep your job search confidential. Make it simple and discreet. Put your target job and industry on the card if you have a very focused job search, or omit that information if you're conducting a broad job search.

710.

Don't flash your resume if you interview with another company in the same building that hosts your current job/company. If the interview must be on-site, proceed to the elevator bank or the floor and act like nothing's out of the ordinary, as if you belong there. If you look guilty, your reason will be abundantly clear to anyone who happens to see you. Going on an interview isn't sinful or felonious; you're just talking to someone about the possibility of a new job.

Another option is to ask for an interview outside the building. If that doesn't work, tell the interviewer that you prefer to sit in an interview room, if possible, rather than the lobby, where passers-by can see you and ask, "What are you doing?"

711. Don't come to work for the first time in three years in a suit that screams "job interview" or put finishing touches on your resume right there at your desk. It's smarter to take a day off than to broadcast your intentions by wearing interview-worthy clothing when that is not your usual garb.

712. Remind the company (during your interview) that your job search is confidential. Ask the hiring manager to refrain from contacting your current employer until you have an offer, and point out that you've marked your existing job "confidential" just as a reminder.

713. Be low-key about your current employer, and never say anything negative (about current or previous employers) on a resume or during an interview. That criticizes your own experience and background. Why did you work at a rotten place for five years? If management was so stupid, why did you stay? Even if your supervisor screamed at you constantly and turned the heat down in the winter and the air conditioning up in the summer, sharing these tales won't gain you points with the hiring manager of another company. Speak well of former employers and hope that they will do the same for you.

714. When your resume reaps interviews, be ethical in the way you handle these appointments. Ideally, take vacation time, especially for an all-day interview. You can have only so many dentist and doctor appointments and deaths in the family before someone figures out that you're scurrying around looking for a job. When you do quit, you want to leave with your former employer liking you and wanting you back. Schedule interviews (if you have a current job) first thing in the morning, during lunchtime, or late in the afternoon. That way, you miss as little work as possible.

715.
Make sure you don't keep resumes on your desk at work because you're the one most likely to leak that you're looking for a job. About 99 percent of the time, that's how an employer finds out. A misplaced confidence does it every time. Of course, it's hard to keep a job search secret if you expect to get a job.

716. Give resumes to only those contacts you truly believe can keep a secret. Of course, you don't need to be paranoid and think everyone is talking about you and your job search. But do remind people that your search is confidential.

717. If you are trying to change career paths, keep track of your resumes when you distribute them far and wide. It's especially hard to keep a job search confidential when you're trying to switch careers because you must network more widely than someone changing jobs within an existing profession. Do talk to lots of people and let them know that your search is confidential. However, don't hand out resumes unless asked. Your resume isn't usually what smooths the way to a career change—it's your network. And the fewer resumes you have floating around, the less hard evidence of your job search.

21.

Don't Blow Your Cover (Letter)

Top every resume with a neatly done, well-composed cover letter that fits the job described in the listing—and highlights your strengths as a candidate for this position. A good cover letter is an extremely important aspect of the job hunt—and an opportunity to impress. All too often, cover letters are dashed off hurriedly, little more than generic efforts. A good cover letter is worded well, flows smoothly, and showcases you as a must-have package of skills and experience that would benefit a company tremendously.

Sell yourself as a great addition to the company. It's worth taking the time to write a rough draft or two until you have something noteworthy. Sometimes a hiring manager looks at the resume and never reads the cover letter at all. Other times, though, the hiring manager reads the cover letter before digging into your resume, which means it's important to play up the attributes that set you apart as an employee. No one knows what you bring to the employment table better than you do, so take every opportunity to reiterate how great your skills and qualities are. A cover letter is just one more vehicle for stating your case persuasively.

Here are some guidelines for writing cover letters:

718.

In the first sentence of your cover letter, clarify why you're an excellent match for the job opening. Get to the point. This is your letter "hook."

719. If you know you're not a strong writer, don't stray too far from a standard cover letter. And when you tweak the opening line that matches your skills to the job listing, have someone look over what you added and make sure it's clear, to the point, and in keeping with the tone and writing style of the rest of the cover letter.

720. By sending a cover letter that you have written specifically for a job listing, you can increase your chances of getting an interview by about 200 percent. Don't try to make something work that isn't appropriate.

721. Think of a good cover letter as a great way to set yourself apart from others who are clamoring for the same position! That will motivate you to write a terrific letter.

722. In your cover letter, be conservative. Don't present yourself as comic relief, the office clown, or a "breath of fresh air" in that you're "unusual." Most hiring managers believe in playing it safe, and unless you're applying for a job as an emcee or TV personality, your uniqueness won't be embraced. (Let the supervisor find out later about your penchant for balancing water bottles, shooting darts at clients, or writing your week's agenda on matchbook covers.)

723.

Make your cover letter one page—no shorter or longer. You won't impress a hiring manager just by being wordy or flowery.

724.

Show enthusiasm for the job. Only stop short of bringing out the big brass band. Don't be reticent about saying how much you would like to work for this company, what a good fit you think the job is, and what you think you do well.

725.

Let the hiring manager know that you're well qualified for the job in question. Spare no words in presenting yourself as a quality candidate who has a good, steady employment history and a sound work ethic. Sound like a standout and the hiring manager will examine your resume carefully.

726. If you have talked to the hiring manager, refer to your conversation with that person in your cover letter. Mention that you are sending your resume, per that individual's request, which puts your resume in a "requested" stack versus a generic stack.

727. Don't go into your special health condition in a cover letter. You can discuss this when you go in for the interview—if it comes up. No one expects every detail of your personal life and health in a cover letter or resume. In fact, the only reason you need to state your health condition at all is if it will affect your ability to perform the job or if you will need special equipment or provisions.

728.
Keep rechecking your cover letter. Every time you tweak one to fit a job listing, have someone read it for you again to make sure that you haven't introduced any new errors. Just because someone proofread it for you the first time around doesn't mean it's mistake-free after several reincarnations to change or add information.

729. Keep details consistent. For the inside addresses (yours and that of the company), use the postal abbreviations (LA, not Louisiana). You want to come across as someone who has been in the working world in recent years; workplace knowledge is important, even if no one admits that it figures into the hiring equation. One woman killed her chances of getting a job by saying she wasn't familiar with the word "teaming" during a preliminary phone interview. To her interviewers, that sent up a red flag: "Old. Out of the loop. Probably low–energy." Unfair assumptions, of course, but resumes and interviews are first–impression moments. That's why you should prepare for every instance in which a prospective employer has a chance to draw conclusions about you as a person or potential employee. Hiring managers are in the business of being judgmental; that's what they get paid for.

730. Give your cover letter a professional look with generous margins (about one inch) and type that's justified on the left (ragged right). Single-space material in the paragraphs and double-space between paragraphs. Give your cover letter a similar feel to that of your resume.

731. When you refer to a company, make sure to use "it" and not "they." A company is a singular word—one thing—and thus, should not be called "they." Example for a cover letter: "My efforts increased market share for Amagood Corporation, and its bottom line was enhanced by 20 percent. As president of the Advertising Federation, I was able to improve the company's image in the community."

732.
Use active voice, not passive, in your cover letter. Example: Very Supportive Company awarded me three Employee of the Month recognitions. Not: I was awarded three Employee of the Month awards by Very Supportive Company.

733. Use parallel sentence structure: "I was responsible for *implementing* programs and *planning* new campaigns." Not: I was responsible for *implementing* programs and *to plan* new campaigns as well."

734. Keep the language simple: "I want to use my skills to benefit your company." Not: "I want to utilize my skills to result in considerable benefits to your company."

735. After finishing a cover letter, you should prune for wordiness. Eliminate expressions such as "finished the work in a timely manner," which could be "finished work on time" or "met deadlines." Why say "on a regular basis" when you can say "regularly?" Or why say, "I would appreciate it so much if you would..." when you can use "Please."

736.

Remember that a cover letter is a one-time thing. You design it to fit the job listing that appealed to you. Don't send a generic-sounding letter because hiring managers will notice—and they won't be motivated to call you for an interview.

737. Cover letters can be used to explain periods of unemployment ("black holes"). If you delve into the non-working years, don't apologize. You can make the most of what you did during a non-working stint. For example, if you took a year off to meditate and go on safari in Africa, talk about the skills gained: self-actualization, travel organizing, and journal-writing. You may also decide to avoid going into that part of your job history altogether.

738. For an international resume, try to find out if the hiring manager prefers a handwritten cover letter. Occasionally, this is the case with international resumes. Check with a company representative to determine the firm's policy in this regard. The handwritten cover letter is a foreign custom that is losing ground. On the other hand, companies based in other countries often ask for your photo, date of birth, and marital status—personal information that American companies can't legally request from employees.

739. Make sure your cover letter explains why you want to relocate and work in another country if it's going to accompany an international resume. That's a logical question in the mind of the hiring manager, so answer it up front. The exception would be if you're leaving the country to avoid hungry creditors, or because you're on probation, or something equally hard to swallow for a potential employer. If wanderlust is your reason for wanting to relocate, emphasize that you have had some long job stints (you don't want to come across as a transient).

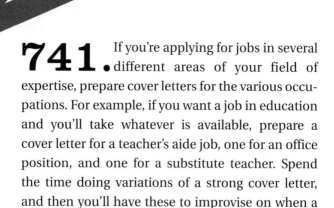

740.
If you don't have a degree, play up skills you have gained, "life lessons" you have acquired, and real-life education that you've gotten on-the-job.

741. If you're applying for jobs in several different areas of your field of expertise, prepare cover letters for the various occupations. For example, if you want a job in education and you'll take whatever is available, prepare a cover letter for a teacher's aide job, one for an office position, and one for a substitute teacher. Spend the time doing variations of a strong cover letter, and then you'll have these to improvise on when a certain job description sounds appealing and you need to mail a cover letter the next day.

742. Include keywords in your cover letter (see chapters 24 and 25 for information on keywords) because you want an Internet scan to get your letter and resume in the door of as many companies as possible.

743.

Research the company so that you know its needs and can refer to them in your cover letter. (Go online to find out.)

744.

Talk about past successes that prove that you're a good fit for the job. The hiring manager or headhunter will be studying this part carefully, so word your descriptions of past successes just right.

745.

Feature prominently the information that explains how you can benefit the company. Make your comments specific rather than general assertions that could apply to any company and any job.

746.

Remember, the hiring manager is reading your resume the same way he reads an ad in the newspaper—he wonders, *What can you do for me?* He wants to know exactly what skills, talents, assets, and qualities you bring to the table, and he doesn't want to have to guess at these things.

747. End your cover letter with a request for an interview, and mention that you will call soon to confirm that the company received your resume. In the end, give your phone number.

748. Check your letter to trim down use of the word "I." Confirm that you have put most of the focus on the company, not on how you will benefit from getting the job.

749.

Never apologize about anything that may adversely affect the hiring manager's decision to grant you an interview.

750. Don't complain about anything. No one wants to hear you grumbling in a cover letter, a resume, an interview, or on the job. If someone asks, "How are you?" he isn't encouraging you to unload a litany of ailments or problems.

751. Don't say why you left a job in your cover letter, or why you're dying to leave. No matter what, it's better not to go into this. If asked during the interview, you can say why you left—unless it was because you hated your boss. That can turn an interview sour very quickly.

752. Don't put your cover letter on the letterhead of the company you're quitting. Many employers consider stationery their property, so what are you doing using it?

753. Avoid language that sounds stilted or old-fashioned, or too slangy or hip. Somewhere between these ends of the spectrum is perfect. Use sophistication, control, and a less-is-more tone.

754. If you know something positive about the company, don't hesitate to toss in a compliment. Example: "Your company interests me because of its excellent reputation for a workplace that is sensitive to employees' needs. I am impressed by your progressive approach to handling the needs of mothers in the workplace by creating a day care facility on-site."

755. Never forget that you're trying to write your cover letter in a way that will help you muscle your way into an interview. Make your last hurrah—the final sentence—come across in a very assertive and positive way. Don't say, "Should you decide to interview me" because that gives the employer the thought "Well, maybe I won't decide to." Instead, say, "I will look forward to talking to you" or "I am confident that my resume will lead to an interview." Express your belief that after reviewing the cover letter and resume, the hiring manager will set up an interview. You have nothing to lose by sounding optimistic and everything to lose by sounding tentative or unsure of yourself.

756. Don't forget to thank the reader for considering your resume and reading your cover letter. Something like this works fine: "Thank you for your time and consideration of my resume."

22.

Lighten Up!

See a funny movie. Ride a bike. Take a walk. Do anything that will keep you from driving friends and family crazy with your nonstop job-hunting tales of woe. If you're sleepless and jobless in Seattle, or anywhere else, say this mantra every morning: "I will find a job. I will use this eight-hour workday on my job search. But I will keep my sense of humor and count my blessings."

Hate your current job? No job at all? Neither is fun, and it's especially trying if you have rent, mortgage payments, car payments, credit cards—and who doesn't? But there are things you can do to make your life easier after you've sent out dozens of resumes and you feel like the city is fairly well blanketed with your name.

Here are some tips for handling the post-resume blues:

757. Tell yourself that you'll get a call if your background is a good fit. Keep in mind that you worked hard on your resume, you're proud of it, and it showcases your skills in a convincing manner.

758.
Don't fret about being on the bottom of the stack; a good resume will rise to the top every time. If you think you haven't put your best foot forward in your resume, look for ways to improve it while you're playing the waiting game. If you have doubts about your resume but you've already sent some out, use the time while you're waiting for responses to revise it a bit.

759. Focus on contacting other employers while you're waiting. Think of unusual ways to scout for work. One example would be finding a list of employers in your field and sending out a personalized cover letter and resume to each one. Tell what you bring to the table and why you would like to be considered when a job opening does turn up. One woman broke into the magazine field (from teaching) by sending her resume to a magazine editor even though there was no job vacancy. In a polished cover letter, the magazine-staffer-wannabe listed reasons (good editing skills, strong background in English, excellent work ethic) that she believed she would be an asset to the business, and asked to be considered. Six months later, she got a note from the editor-in-chief: "Please call to set up an interview. We may have something for you." If she hadn't caught the editor's eye during a no-job-opening period, they would have opened up the interview process and reviewed hundreds of candidates' resumes; as it was, she "had them from hello."

760. Network while waiting for interviews. And don't stick to your own field exclusively. People know lots of people, and you never know when even your hairstylist may come across a client who needs your skills. Remember, people tell their hairstylists, masseuses, and personal trainers everything; they're the best networking people around.

761.

Don't neglect the word-of-mouth in clubs, churches, etc. Spread the message that you're job-hunting, and ask people to remember you when they hear of something.

762. Remember one important thing: While it is true that your resume-sitting-on-that-supervisor's-desk is paramount in your mind, it's a low priority in that person's daily workload of pressing items.

763. If you see an ad for a job that has nothing to do with your own past job responsibilities but sounds appealing, don't let your resume hold you back. Sit down and start writing. Skills you've used on other jobs usually have a way of crossing over and serving you well even in a different territory. You just have to be creative in your way of thinking about how your abilities would apply to the new-and-different job.

764.

Mull over the idea of relocating to broaden your job opportunities. For some folks, this sounds like extreme job searching, but people move all the time in order to find better positions. Consider it, even if relocation is your last choice.

765.

Start an exercise program or join a health club during the waiting period; take a long walk or run every morning before you sit down to work on your job search.

766.

Consider having a makeover. Sometimes what's holding a person back from getting hired may be a simple image problem. You may be the smartest, most capable candidate represented in the stack of resumes, but will your image hold up when they ask you to come in for an interview? Try to find an honest friend or relative and ask this question: Do I need a fashion, hair, or makeup update in order to make the best impression on a job interview? That opens the door for a friend or relative to offer thoughts on ways you can be at your absolute best by the time your interview day arrives.

767. Get rid of preconceived notions about what should be happening when a hiring manager reviews your resume: "If that person has half a brain, he'll spot me as the top candidate!" "I'm wearing my handlebar mustache no matter what anyone tells me!" "I like my tattoos, and I'm not covering them up with a long-sleeved shirt for an interview." Individualism is fine, but when it comes to competing for a job, be realistic. You probably have no idea what kind of person will interview you (conservative? wacky? friendly? adventuresome?), so why not play it safe and make sure that you don't stand out in any negative way. We all know that some people don't like tattoos and body piercing, and one of those may be your interviewer. Why flaunt that you're unconventional (or anti-establishment) unless you're absolutely sure that will help you get the job? Most positions require a certain amount of being conventional and following rules, usually including a dress code. Show the hiring manager going in that you're willing to be a cooperative and law-abiding employee.

768. Don't forget that you always have other options if the resume you sent doesn't get you the job you want. You can take on new responsibilities in your current job that will pave your way into another part of the company or a different kind of position. You can change professions. You can do the same kind of work you're now doing but find a different company that offers greater opportunities for promotions and financial rewards.

769.

Practice positive self-talk: "It's a good idea to look for a job that interests me more, that offers a situation in which I'll feel more appreciated or more adept, and my expectations for finding such a job are founded in reality. If I do all the right things that job-hunters should do, I will find something I like."

770. Work on improving your skills in areas you previously considered "too scary." An example would be public speaking. Fear of public speaking can hold some people back in their jobs and conquering this fear can open doors for new job opportunities. So look at your particular job situation and decide if learning how to speak in front of groups would benefit you. Or, put time and effort into taking care of some other deficiency, such as becoming a higher-tech employee. When you decide you want to beef up a skill, think over the challenge. Expect to succeed, get the tools to do so, and you're halfway there.

771. Work on overcoming your job-interview anxiety. It's perfectly normal to feel jittery about an upcoming interview that matters a great deal to you, but there are things you can do to decompress. See ideas in this chapter.

772. Vow to make your next job experience your best. If your work efforts have gone largely unnoticed in the past, perhaps it's because you make the common workplace mistake of being too "low-profile." If your supervisor and department can barely tell that you're there, you won't be considered a big asset. Thus, no one will see a ripple when you get laid off, right? It's up to you to make sure you are viewed as a key employee; your boss may not mind seeing some people resign, but not you! Plan to take the next job you have (or the current one) with the attitude that you're there to make a difference: have a great attitude, improve the bottom line, establish excellent rapport with coworkers, go to work every day, and become known as a cooperative, easygoing, and enthusiastic employee. Then, if you ever decide to quit, you can expect to see some weeping and wailing going on; your departure will be viewed as a mini-disaster!

773.

While you're waiting to get a job interview, put yourself out there on your current job, or in your job search. Initiate projects, do volunteer work, help people who need help. Then revise your resume to include the latest and greatest things you have done in these endeavors. Grow yourself. The day you think you know everything necessary to be a great employee is the day you start to go stagnant.

774. Defuse the stress you feel over being in a job you hate. Look at the realities. It's only natural to feel sad, frustrated, and angry if you've experienced a workplace betrayal or your boss is an overbearing monster. Share your anxiety with someone at home, not at work, and talk through your frustrations. Ask yourself: What's the worst thing that can happen if I don't get another job and I'm forced to endure this job for another year? The answer: You won't die, you won't go crazy, and you probably won't get fired.

775. Think survival. Avoid bickering with your boss or coworkers and admit that although it's truly a tough situation, you've made it through rough things in the past, and you will survive this job, too. If the situation becomes so unbearable you want to quit without having another job lined up, think about this one for a while. And then, if you have no choice because you're so miserable, exit with grace and waste no time getting your resume out, starting the very next day.

776.
Keep your skills sharp. Focus on continuing to learn new things you can use in your profession.

777. Don't demonize the job hunt. Look at it as something everyone does at one time or another—and remind yourself that few people have sought jobs without facing roadblocks and frustrations. You're in the same situation as millions of other people. Take some degree of comfort in that.

778. Consider keeping a journal of your job search. You can make it sad, funny, hopeful, silly—whatever you want to write down in your book. This is excellent therapy for your stressed-out psyche, and your journal won't ever tire of listening to you. As a fringe benefit, you may gain inspiration or motivation, or find a springboard to a new job idea.

779. Prepare for the layoff you see coming when rumors are flying through the company grapevine. Merely sending out resumes isn't the only thing you can do. Come up with Plans A, B, and C. Consider trying a career move that's something you've only dreamed of in the past—maybe a hobby that's your passion. Don't quit your day job (you need to pay your bills), but you can start attending night classes to get training or credentials in the field you want to enter. Network with people who do things you've never tried, and see if their work sounds interesting to you. Reframe your job search: When people ask if being laid off terrifies you, tell them, "Not really because I look at this as an exciting time in my life. I'm going to try to do something I've always wanted to do."

780. Give yourself permission to feel bad occasionally, but put a time limit on moments of self-pity. Spend your new free time (after being fired or laid off) on your job search.

781. Address your spirituality. This helps many people to cope better with rough times. When life seems nonsensical, take to the bunker of your spiritual self and seek a peaceful state of mind that will carry you through the storm.

782. Don't pretend that joblessness is fun—it isn't. Nor is it unimportant. Face your situation head-on, and don't be satisfied with having three resumes in the mail when you could have ten resumes reaching destinations where job openings exist. Confront the reality and make moves to become gainfully employed as soon as possible.

783.

Write a new life script. Decide what you would like to see happen in your life in the next two years and list ideas for making those things happen.

784. Avoid taking the negative position that you're a casualty of a bad economy, or a victim of the job-hunting wars. Think of yourself as being in charge of what happens to you (to some degree, anyway), and expect to have a satisfying, productive life. Smile, laugh, and look for ways to get out and do things that will make you feel vibrant and alive.

785. Don't give in to the temptation to hide. Becoming a recluse won't help. Being around people is almost always invigorating, and socializing makes most of us feel more hopeful when we're looking for a job.

786.

Visualize yourself being successful in the job race. Imagine how you will go in to interview, impress the hiring manager, and get a job offer. You know that your confidence and skills will make you a shoo-in for the position you want. Empower yourself to be the kind of person who can make things happen.

787.
Close your eyes and relax; breathe deeply. Imagine yourself in a setting that is remarkable for its peacefulness. Float there and enjoy the serenity. Think of yourself as an unflappable, secure person who will soon have a good job, with all the worry and stress behind you.

788. Work on getting your credit record shaped up if you need to. A bad debt history can hurt when you're job shopping because some employers ask permission to check your credit rating (and some do this surreptitiously). If they find that you've piled up lots of credit-card debt you couldn't pay, the assumption may be that you'll be similarly disorganized and unaccountable on the job.

23.

Seek Professional Resume Help If You Need It

Maybe you've tried everything in the world, but you can see that your resume is less than impressive when you peer into the eyes of people who read it. Don't worry—there are plenty of options out there if you can't do it yourself. You can get outside help in preparing a resume, and, in fact, you probably should seek resume help if:

- You can't stand to write anything.
- You're pretty sure that you're an awful writer.
- You don't have a handy friend or relative to read and critique your resume.

- You don't have time to turn out a brand-new resume.
- You want to make sure the resume you turn out will maximize your skills and background and get you the most incredible job you've ever had.
- Your current resume isn't generating interviews and you've been sending it out for months. (Something's wrong!)
- You've never written a resume before.
- You have a dicey work history that "needs special help."
- You're job-challenged, having little experience that really amounts to anything.
- You're reentering the job market after raising children, sailing the Caribbean, or getting bored with retirement. Anything that has taken you away from the mainstream marketplace is cause for seeking someone's help in steering you back into the working world. Things change in as little as five or ten years.

Here are tips to remember when you seek help in writing a resume:

789. Understand that you will pay for help, but that it's money well spent. The fee for having a professional write your resume ranges from about $100 to $500 and up. In some cases, a firm is so sure that its resumes will reap results that it guarantees the work—your new resume will generate interviews for you in thirty days or the writer will rewrite or reformat your resume for free.

790. Find out the name of a resume professional by checking with a career consultant or a recruiter.

791.
If you know someone in human resources for any company, ask that person for a referral to a resume professional.

792. Find a resume writer by checking with your university student center bulletin board or newsletter, which usually has listing of resume preparation services. In some states, a university's career services office provides resume writing at a very low cost for alumni.

793. Check with friends who may know some resume professionals they can recommend.

794. Try to go it alone by using the template Resume Wizard (Microsoft Word).

795. Find a friend or relative who is a good writer and ask him to help you write an excellent resume.

796. Hire someone from a clerical service to turn out a new resume. Here, you will get clerical processing of your resume—not full-service resume writing, typically. Also, you may only get a paper resume when you probably need both paper and online versions.

797. Hire a professional resume writer online. Try the following web sites: http://polishedresumes.com, http://proven resumes. com, http://www.my-resume-writer.com, or http://www.parw.com.

The last of these is the web site for the Professional Association of Resume Writers and Career Coaches, which can provide you with names of resume professionals in your city and state.

798. Don't assume that a resume writer's certification means that you'll get a great resume. Look at samples, study them carefully, and make your decision based on the actual goods. You may also find a perfectly good resume writer who has never bothered with certification because he has all the business he can handle (see chapter 15 for ideas on ways to show appreciation to those who aid in your job search).

799. Try an online resume builder such as Monster Resume Center, which provides in-depth resume help, from career advice to job listings, resume tips, and creation.

800. Buy a form at a business-supply store and use it to prepare your resume. Business stores have special resume-making forms, which work well if you have a general idea of what you want to get across and how to do it.

801.
Organize the material on your job history before you present it to the pro resume writer. Don't make him have to decide what's important and what's not. Highlight items that should be emphasized, and ask the writer if he agrees with you.

802. If you have chosen to use a resume writer, ask if that person knows how to articulate what type of position you're looking for and how to back that up with evidence you can do the job.

803. Find out if the resume firm accepts credit cards—that's a good sign that the business is legitimate.

804. Watch for a generic quality in the resume writer or firm. You can detect that this is a problem if no one seems interested in talking to you to get your unique story.

805.
When a resume professional shows you samples, read them for clarity and professionalism and check out the appearance: paper, printing, design. The overall look and feel should be crisp, concise, and clean.

806. Don't let a resume writer bowl you over by showing you resumes he has prepared in a large-page format, placed in expensive binders. That's not what a hiring manager wants to see, so why pay extra for it? In fact, for most hiring managers, that's a turn-off.

807. Watch out for fanciful approaches. A resume writer may say she does something extraordinary and sell you bells and whistles, but it's going to be your problem when the hiring manager opens your envelope, finds a resume bedecked in flowery artwork and exclamation marks, and is less than thrilled.

808.
Ask how long the resume firm has been in business (the longer, the better). Check with your local office of the Better Business Bureau to find out if there have been any complaints filed against the resume firm you're considering.

809. Find out if the resume firm will talk to you free for the initial visit. When you're merely seeking some idea of what they can do for you, there should be no charge. However, don't expect to use this brief consult as an opportunity to spell out your entire job history. An up-front consultation can be face-to-face or on the phone, but don't take more than ten minutes of the person's time.

810. Fill out the form required by resume firms, but also request a meeting with the writer. Otherwise, you'll get nothing more than a boilerplate resume, which won't do you much good.

811. Make sure you speak with the person who will do the writing, not the office manager. You want to make sure that you can develop rapport with this individual. A writer who won't look at you or can't communicate well isn't likely to be able to get your message across in a resume.

812. Ask the resume writer how many resumes he has written, not how many the company has turned out.

813. In the initial meeting, specify your particular job-search deficiency or problem as you perceive it—and ask the writer what she would do (in general terms) to handle that kind of dilemma when writing a resume for you. Other initial meeting tips:

- Ask the resume writer to make sure that your resume has plenty of keywords that a company scanner will pick up.
- Ask the resume writer if he can prepare a resume that you can email.
- Tell the resume writer what your strengths are and how those strengths have been recognized in past job (awards, praise, raises, promotions).
- Give the resume writer something to work with. Explain experiences that make you special and strengths that make you a good job candidate.

814. Ask for reassurance that the resume writer can give you substance over style. Say that you want a resume that sells you, not pretties you up.

815.

Ask for a flat rate (longer isn't better in resumes so you don't want to pay by the page). Also, inquire about other charges. Ask how much the company will charge to modify your resume once it's written. Ask what the fee is if you return for small changes in two months. Find out how much the writer/firm will charge you for extra copies of your resume.

816.
Don't be unfair and use a visit with a resume writer just to find out what he or she knows that you don't know.

817.
Make sure to ask for samples of resumes before you sign up or pay (unless the person is a professional writer you already know and trust).

818.
If you hire a firm or individual to write your resume, find out what the agreement specifies: Your approval of the final product? One copy of the resume? Ten? A revision if the resume fails to work for you within a specified period?

819. Find out what's going to happen if you pick up your resume and it's a big disappointment. What can you do if you discover that your resume written by "professional" is full of mistakes and typos? Did anyone guarantee you that it would be typo-free and grammatically correct?

820. Caution the professional resume writer not to get overly ambitious and inflate your resume so that you can't even recognize the job candidate being described, much less live up to the image. Some resume writers get overzealous, especially when the job candidate has next to nothing in the way of job history, education, or skills. Make it clear to the resume writer that you don't want fabrications.

821. Let the resume writer make the final call on iffy inclusions. For example, you may think your years as a rodeo clown make you a good candidate for a job as a fashion-show emcee, but the resume writer contends that big shoes and a fake red nose make you more laughable than lovable. In such cases, listen to the expert who is more objective about your background than you are.

24.

Know the Pros and Cons of E-Resumes

Job seekers face a sophisticated world when it comes to job hunting, and nothing has changed the scenario more than the Internet. The advantage of this new wave is that you can enlarge your spectrum of job possibilities simply by extending your job search online. Only a decade ago, that was an unusual way to job hunt, but today, the Internet is a staple of the jobless and the restless. If you're not using the Internet to help you find a job, you're missing out on a huge chance to become gainfully employed—pronto.

Many companies now rely on scanning technology to read resumes, and some firms routinely ask that you email your resume to them for perusal. If you don't know how to respond to the request for an electronic resume, you may get marked off the list of candidates early on.

Mostly, we're past the day of having to simplify your resume into plain-text to get it through computer lines. Today, a resume can be both light-and-portable and good-looking. Many employers screen resumes online, and you can attract their attention and get in the race for jobs you may not even know exist.

Tips on e-resumes, and some of their pros and cons, include the following:

822. Remember that most medium-size and large companies process resumes by computer because it's efficient, accurate, fast, and gives the competitive edge.

823. Follow protocol for e-resumes. Emailing resumes has distinct protocol, and for maximum results, follow the rules. When the directions say to send the resume in ASCII or Text Only format, make sure you send the resume that way. (Pronounced "AS-key, this acronym is short for American Standard Code for Information Exchange.) If you are directed to attach the resume as a Word or WordPerfect document, do so. If you are asked to cut-and-paste your resume into blocks, use the ASCII or Text Only version for best results.

824. Understand corporate America's viewpoint on e-resumes. The ease of retrieval and storage of resumes, from the company's perspective, is a huge factor, and that's why it's very important for you to become e-resume savvy. Think of it: the hiring manager receives your electronic resume right there at her desktop without having to pick up the phone, check the company's mail, or lift a finger. Furthermore, the resume can be easily stored in a file folder or database, ready for a hiring manager to retrieve.

825.

Understand the logistics: a computer reads your resume with a device known as a scanner or optical recognition system. You have to ensure that your resume is easy for the computer to read. (See chapter 25 to instructions on how to make that happen.)

826. Don't argue the pros and cons of e-resumes if a hiring manager requests one. She obviously thinks there are more pros than cons, and that's all you need to know. Being contentious on the subject won't win you any points; worse, you present yourself as trouble before you've even been invited for an interview!

827. If an employer asks you to email a resume, agree to do it even if you don't know how—and then make it your job to find out how, and do it correctly.

828.
Email your resume if the employer says "either way is fine—send us a resume we can scan or email your resume."

829. Expect some companies to balk at your sending a resume as an attachment. Many employers, because of viruses, simply won't open attachments. Also, you may not be able to send a resume by attachment because of incompatibility of Internet service providers, computer platforms, or software. To be safe, copy and paste your resume after your cover letter email note, to suit the company's preference.

830. Understand what an e-resume is. It's designed for computer use and can be sent over the Internet, as well as saved on your hard drive or a computer disk. Search engines can find your e-resume (the electronic document), and it can be checked/searched for keywords included in it. Also, you can print it out (hard copy).

831. A company gets e-resumes from its web site, through online job banks, and via email, and often hard copy resumes are scanned into the company database via a scanning device in a computer. When someone manually enters your resume into the company's database, the keyer may do some adjusting of the material found there.

832. Don't muddy the issue of excellence. Sometimes you may be asked to pare down your resume when making it an e-resume, but it still has to be perfect, typo-free, concise, and excellent.

833. Understand the keyword search ranking theory, and keep this in mind when preparing an e-resume. (See chapter 25 for more information.) When resumes are read through a scanner, someone in the company has designated keywords or phrases the computer should search for. Depending on how often and where in the resume the words appear, the resume is ranked among others according to the closeness of the match.

834.

Understand that using keywords means sticking your neck out. If you flaunt the word "Sales," you need to know the assumptions that employers will make when they know you have sales experience. They assume that you know how to develop new business and introduce new products, be a strong closer, and court/handle/cater to customers.

835. As you prepare your e-resume, imagine a company that is doing keyword searches of hundreds, even thousands, of resumes in hopes of finding a candidate who has experience in the things it requires.

836. Take advantage of one gigantic benefit of e-resumes—the ease of speedy response. When you see an attractive job listed, it's certainly faster to send a resume over the Internet versus printing out a copy, addressing an envelope, and licking/sticking a stamp. Putting your resume on the Internet takes only a few keystrokes and a few seconds.

837. Don't forget the confidential aspect of e-resume use. Remember, when you send a fax to a phone number, you have no idea whose eyes will see your resume. Your resume could sit on the fax machine for an hour, and everyone on the fourth floor may glance at it. But when you send your resume to an email address, you're more likely to have your resume deposited directly into a folder or database, which prevents casual perusing by a few coworkers or the entire company.

838.

Take advantage of the money-saving aspect of e-resumes. When you send a resume via the Internet, it costs you nothing but your time and psychic energy. When you send a resume by regular mail, you have to pay for the bond paper, matching envelope, and a postage stamp.

839.

An e-resume gives you the ability to respond immediately to positions on job boards. Job boards are online want ads, and about 90 percent of the time, you will be expected to email your responses.

840.

Visit the web site of the company you want to work for and see if the hiring manager accepts e-resumes. You'll probably see a fax number and mailing address on the web site, too. Today, all employers are expected to use the Internet and often submit information online.

841.

Use the e-resume to contact a recruiting firm via the Internet. Just like job boards and some companies, recruiting firms prefer to receive resumes online. The electronic form makes it easier to store and search for resumes.

842.

Know the downside of e-resumes. The flip side of ease and economy of sending is that more people respond to Internet ads for those reasons, too. The result is that companies and web sites are deluged with responses and resumes, which can make it difficult to shine amid a bounty of responses.

843.

Sharpen your e-resume with mega-competition in mind. By the time the hiring manager reads resume number 532, he may be bleary-eyed, disinterested, and impossible to impress.

844. Remember that email glitches can gum up the works. You can carefully send your resume into cyberspace and have it fail to arrive, without receiving any indication of the failure. More likely, though, you'll get an error message, indicating that it didn't get delivered. Some systems create an error message, such as "undeliverable mail or "mail daemon," with an explanation for the lack of completion.

845.

If you receive a system error, check that the email address is correct, re-send the resume, and then confirm receipt by calling the person to whom you sent the resume. The point is this: You have no guarantee that your email will reach its appointed destination, so it's up to you to make sure that happens.

846. Be careful. Complicating the picture is a new development in the world of devious computer hackers.

847. Save each version of your e-resume, clearly marked with the name of the company it went to, so that you can find that version again and have it nearby when you're interviewing.

848. Typically, you modify each e-resume to fit the specifics of the job description that you're applying for, and you want to make sure that you can pull up the exact version of your resume you sent to the company or recruiter. Tag each version sent with a clear name, such as: Smith.Jane.TwethAssoc. Make it clear to you, but don't make the name too clear to others. Also, choose a generic name to save your resume. Don't use: Smith.Jane.lastemployeromitted.

849. When in doubt, print out the e-resume you sent to a company and make notes. File it for future reference and follow-up.

850.
Use folders. Save each e-resume version and whom it was sent to in a computer file folder. Keep a detailed record in a "Job Search" or "Resume Sent" folder. Copy your cover letter and save that into the file folder as well.

851. Follow record-keeping rules. If you keep good records, you will be able to contact the recipients of resumes you've sent. After you have sent the resume via email or attached it to a job posting on a company web site or job board, follow up with the recipient within forty-eight hours. Don't expect to have your call returned (remember the huge response that ads and job boards get). If you don't receive a callback, phone again after another forty-eight hours. This time, if no one returns your call, try again in a week to see if the resume was received.

852. Understand PDF resumes. PDF is a common form of posting resumes. You can create PDF files from Word documents and text files. Advantages are: they carry no viruses, they retain formatting when the employer prints them out, and they can't be altered, and are therefore secure. To create such a file, you need a computer program called Adobe Acrobat, and to read a .pdf file requires the Adobe Acrobat Reader. Download these and you're ready to go. See www.adobe.com/products/acrobat/main.html.

853. What if you could beam your resume to someone across the room at a networking function, or in an office across the city? You *can*—with the high-tech option called the Beamer (BM-80 PVS), a phone video station that resembles a little picture frame. Basically, this picture-phone by Vialta can transform a standard phone into a visual one, but the problem is, your potential resume recipient must have a Beamer, too, or a similar contraption. A quick version of your resume can be read on someone's PDA (personal digital assistant) or digital phone. Picturephoning could be the wave of the future, and it's easy to imagine enthusiastic networkers bombarding hiring managers with resumes via Beamers.

854.

Business-card your resume. Another new idea is to have a mini version of your resume on a business card that you can hand out at networking functions. Obviously, it would have to be a condensed version, but who wouldn't find this cool?

855. Set up a web-resume. A glam trend that may get bigger in years to come is the web-resume, whereby you post your resume on your own web site and provide links to examples of your work. This puts your resume on the road map for many recruiters, who will find it on various search engines. Let's say you're an artist who wants to post a resume and links to various art galleries' web sites where your work is shown. The web-resume would be a real winner in a case like this. Having the options of fun graphics and music, you open yourself up to infinite possibilities with a web-resume, which may turn off hiring managers in subdued and ultra-sophisticated professions, but may wow those in arts, media, and entertainment. Basically, a web-resume complete with links amounts to an e-portfolio; you can strut your stuff for interested onlookers. The downside, of course, is that setting up one of these takes lots of time and expertise (or the money to pay someone to create your web site for you).

856. Do a broadcast resume. There you are, speaking and gesturing in living color, and you're broadcasting this into the office of a hiring manager by putting it on a disk or videotape and sending it in.

857.

Send out an e-newsletter to help your job search. You have information to share, and you're willing to do this. But along with that generosity, you're transmitting your credentials for interested lookers. Let's say you're a publicist who wants a job with a department store. You write a newsletter that gives people in all professions substantial tips on marketing their services, and in the bargain you can solicit for leads on jobs for yourself. Pitch your skills, and ask for work. Send it out as an email newsletter.

25.

Create Your E-Resume

You send an e-resume through a computer. When someone refers to an e-resume, he may be talking about a file that you send as an email attachment, a resume within an email message, a resume you submit to a company's web site, or a resume that you post on an Internet job site (Monster, for example). The scannable resume, on the other hand, turns into an e-resume only after someone takes your regular paper resume and scans it into a database.

858. Understand that in today's fast-moving world of software and high-tech developments, the way resumes are sent and handled is constantly changing, so you have to stay abreast of what's happening in the job-search realm when you're on the prowl for a new position.

859. Get a feel for how the scanning process works. Your resume is placed on a glass inside the scanner to allow an OCR (optical character reading) program to read the resume—then it's stored away in the company's database. When a position opens up, an employer tells the computers the position keywords (these refer to the main skills/traits, experience, and education the job requires). Any resumes that are matches are found in seconds; these fall in order of most matches to medium-number matches, etc.

860. Understand applicant tracking systems (ATS). Basically, applicant tracking is software that handles a company's job postings and its collection of resumes to match a candidate to a job. Applicant management does the ATS business and more; it actually screens job candidates online.

861. Understand online screening (AKA pre-employment screening), which means that employers can do research on you with the greatest of ease and discover things that previously could be kept firmly under wraps and often not revealed until after you were hired.

862. Make sure you understand the drift of the online screening process. This information will help you prepare a better e-resume. It starts when you visit the company's web site and answer questions, feeding your information into the computer mix so the company can consider you for a job. Examples: Do you have at least five years' experience as a graphic artist? Have you ever directed a magazine art staff of four or more employees? Is your salary range $75,000–$100,000 per year? Do you have a four-year degree? Your answers are used for first-round screening; give the wrong answer and your resume is a goner in competition for this position.

863.

Online screening can include background checks, credit reports, employment history, education verification, arrest records, bankruptcy records, medical records, driving record, address history, and more. Some states, however, don't allow release of this kind of information unless you give signed permission. It is useful to do an advance check to make sure your credit report is up-to-date and accurate.

864.

Know the facts: As a job hunter today, you need to have:

- A pretty resume, full-tilt in fancy format and sales punch. This is the fancy Microsoft Word or WordPerfect version that has all the fonts, bullet points, and italics you want—the resulting visual reflects you, the job candidate. It's the version you send as an attachment or cut-and-paste into a box on an application, or print out hard copies to mail. This is also the one that's referred to as "fully formatted." This resume must be visually impressive to a hiring manager who is holding it in his hands and perusing it. Make copies and hand it out as needed.

- A plain-Jane sure-to-scan resume (you've eliminated italics, graphics, etc. to make sure it scans well).
- A keyword-laden resume that is scannable.
- An ASCII version of your resume (converted from your scannable one) with a keyword summary at the top to sell your skills package. ASCII (American Standard Code for Information Interchange) is the plain format you usually use to send a resume to web sites, job boards, etc. ASCII is the plainest version of your resume; you achieve this format by typing your resume and saving it as "text only." After you have saved your document, click on SAVE, then pull down the menu-SAVE AS TYPE-"Text only." (By the way, after you save as "Text only," expect your resume to appear in the font Courier or Courier New, easy for a computer to read.)
- The ability to send an e-resume by email and to copy and paste vital data into employers' e-forms that you find on their web sites.
- A willingness to revise your e-resume quickly when you see a job listing that attracts you.

865. Know the ways to make sure your resume negotiates the cyberspace galaxy safely. When emailing your resume, make sure that you use a format that the company can accept. If what you send is incompatible with the company's software, that's the end of your applying process—your resume is history. Why didn't you call to find out what the hiring manager prefers?

866.

Even though one-page resumes will always be popular and preferred, you can make your resume longer than one page and it will still work for scanning purposes.

867. Always send originals. Use paper that is clean and that makes your resume easy to read.

868. Make sure the black ink is dark enough. If you're low on toner, replace it before you do resumes.

869. Don't use unfamiliar abbreviations.

870. Don't print on the back of each sheet.

871. Justify your e-resume on the left.

872. Get ready for a numbers game: the more keywords in your resume that match up, the better your chances of getting your foot in the door. An employer who's ready to hire can specify a type of experience or skill he needs for a position, and that info is used to sort the resumes stored in the company's database. The matches pop up and are printed for the hiring manager's perusal. Elements that such searches target are job titles, certain skills, areas of experience, specific types of education, and industry buzzwords.

873. Just because your resume can be scanned doesn't automatically mean that it has the keywords a scanner is looking for. The keywords an employer wants to find are what make your resume rise to the top and become a contender.

Recognize that resume scanning allows an employer to send out a call for an employee who has certain skills. Perhaps the skills list would include teaming, decision–making, strategic planning, and crisis management. This means, obviously, that your resume must have some of these power keywords. A scannable resume, then, is just a paper resume that's become an image after being scanned into a computer. The scanner in the computer is programmed to pull out the high points from each of these images. The resume and its summary are then filed until a hiring manager decides to conduct a search to look for a specific candidate for a job opening. The computer zeros in on keywords and comes up with the most qualified candidates, ranking them in order. The catch is that you won't look like a highly qualified candidate, even if you are, if you fail to include the keywords for your profession that the computer will recognize.

Realize that every field of endeavor has keywords, and leaving them out will seriously cut down on your job possibilities, even if it just so happens that you actually are superb at decision-making, strategic planning, and crisis management. Maybe you simply worded it differently on your resume, but unfortunately, the savvier candidate will get the interview.

874.

Right below your name and address, place your keyword summary (that's a list of your qualifications stated in keyword phrases).

875.

Find good keywords in job listings, company brochures or other information, industry jargon, and Internet information on job searches.

Look for the skills in each job listing you read, and use some of these nouns as keywords in your resume. That way, you show what a close match you are for the position listed. For example, let's say a magazine is advertising for a senior editor, and the skills it mentions are extensive writing experience, copy editing, and proofreading. If you want to draw attention to yourself, make sure these keywords appear in your resume's keyword summary.

For example, if you are in upper management, your resume should include some of these keywords: decision-making, job-offering, organizational leadership, profitability improvement, corporate administration, business development, profit-and-loss responsibility, problem-solving, corporate administration, teaming.

876. You can put your keywords under the heading "Professional Qualifications." This sets them apart and may ensure that resume-scanning picks them up. The upside? It shows that you know that companies scan resumes. Downside? It makes your resume look "canned" and too much like that of the next candidate in line.

877. Remember that keywords belong in your cover letter and interview thank-you letter too, not just your resume.

878. Use some keywords in the first line or two of the resume to illustrate early on the value that you bring to the company. Also, mesh keywords into the resume's body.

879. Make sure that you know the meaning of the keywords in your resume in case they come up during your interview. If you say that you're good at teaming, you'd better know what it is. What's important is to use keywords that send the message that you're a great match for the kind of position you want.

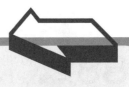

880.

Understand the latest developments. To confuse matters, scannable resumes are on the way out, and so is the plain-text resume (no one ever liked the way these looked, anyway). At the same time, don't scrap your text version or your scannable resume because someone may ask for one or the other at some point. What's on the horizon is later-greater technology for handling resumes, which is making resume scanning outmoded. Today, some jobs and companies' web portals invite you to attach your resume in its full-gloried format. It's very slick and eliminates the downside of resume scanning, which is the errors that sometimes occur during conversion.

881.

Take care of your resume's arrival by finding out what the employer wants you to do. Call or email someone in the human resources department and ask if you can submit your resume via email. If the person says that's OK, then ask if an attachment sent in MS Word or WordPerfect will work. And do they convert the attachment to text? If you discover that the company will be taking your resume and converting it to text, go ahead and do that yourself; send your resume as an ASCII file. Otherwise, you run the risk of their "converting" making your resume look unusual by altering line lengths or adding deep indents.

882. To fill out an e-form on a company web site, you cut and paste the modules of your plain text resume into the company's form. The employer may also have some specific instructions. After you're finished, you just hit "Send." The downside of the e-form is that you don't get a chance to brag about your intangible plusses; you simply answer questions the employer poses.

883.

When submitting your resume by email, use the subject line to list the job title you're applying for in order to get someone's attention.

884. Send your resume to web sites such as Guru (www.guru.com), a site where writers register to be informed of freelance projects, and then the site emails notes periodically when something comes in. The email goes like this: "We have received a project titled 'Copywriter Needed' (ID 666) that matches your profile. Scroll down to view the project details. If you choose to express interest in this project, we will release your bid, proposal, name, and contact information to the employer." Then, Guru walks the writer through the steps in bidding on the project by using the link to log in and then clicking on the project title. Employers pay via Guru web site's billing service. These projects range from infomercial copywriting to a long-term commitment to edit a book or write a multi-phase project.

There are many similar free or fee-based sites that can act as job agents for you. You fill in information, and the result is a profile of the kinds of jobs you're interested in: type of work, title, industry, salary range, and place. After providing your email address so you can be contacted when something comes up, you never need to give the site another thought. Then, when your "agent" lets you know about a job, it's your call whether or not you would like your resume considered.

885. Don't top the email cover sheet with just "Process Control Engineer" when you could actually sell yourself with "Experienced chemical engineer whose top skills include excellence in the areas of writing code, handling chemical-plant troubleshooting, and serving as a group lead." You will also include a cover letter and the e-resume.

886.

Don't use a job title in your career objective—it's better to say that you're interested in the industry and avoid references to a title.

887. Put your name on each page of what you send. Whether yours is an electronic resume or a paper resume, your name should be on each piece of paper. If your resume is misplaced or the electronic transfer is jumbled, at least your name will be easy to find.

888. Use regular white 8½ x 11-inch paper (colored and/or textured paper won't work).

889. Use only black typeface, and choose a standard font. Good choices are sans-serif fonts such as Arial and Helvetica.

890. Put your name in type that's larger than the body type—but no larger than 18 point. For the body of your resume, use a type size of 12. Do not use anything smaller than 10 point or larger than 14 point. Remember that 8- or 9-point type is too little. Many scanners can't read type that's very small, huge, or decorative.

891. Use 14- or 16-point type for section headers and for your name at the top, if that's the look you want. Be sure that you don't vary type sizes throughout the resume.

892. Don't use a two-column format.

893. Don't use parentheses if possible.

894. Keep tab use to a minimum.

895. Don't use graphics, and avoid use of bullets, arrows, etc. because when you convert your resume from the regular Word or WordPerfect to Text Only, you lose most of the formatting. Bullets and other formatting will be converted to a very plain version that a computer can read better.

896. Avoid the use of brackets anywhere in your resume.

897. If you're mailing your resume, don't fold it. Send it flat in a large envelope.

898. Put only your name on the top line (very important!). Put your address below your name, not beside or above it.

899. Stick to well-known "titles" for section headers: Summary of Qualifications, Professional Experience, Accomplishments, Work History, Education, Awards and Honors, Certifications, etc. Get too creative and the scanner may not be able to recognize the terms.

900. Use all caps for section headers to make them stand out.

901. Make sure that the email address you put on your resume doesn't sound lightweight or silly. If it does, list a different one (get one free from Microsoft Hotmail).

902. Avoid using italics, script, shadowing, number signs, boxes, symbols, and vertical or horizontal lines.

903. Avoid slashes, boldface, and underlining or shadowing/shading.

904. Avoid using a typewriter or dotmatrix printer to do a scannable resume.

905. Don't fax unless that's the only way the employer will receive resumes.

906.
Do include a cover letter just in case the company's scanning system can use it.

907. When you're ready to send your e-resume, on your email cover page, put the recipient's name, refer to the position, and tell how you discovered the job listing.

26.

Know What Employers Consider Resume Turn-Ons, Turn-Offs

It's good to be aware of what hirers consider major resume coups and screw-ups. Almost everyone in business today can offer some strong-held feelings on what he likes and hates in a resume. Expounding on these subjects are some bosses and entrepreneurs who know how to find good employees—below they answer the question "When looking at resumes, what turns you on and what turns you off?"

908.

Leon Hall, entertainer and emcee: "I don't like to see misspelled words; rambling, lengthy, non-succinct responses or explanations; inaccuracy in dates; and a lack of good and pertinent references. What I do like to see are the opposite of these things."

909.

Angela Clark, co-owner of Court Record Research: "A turn-off is a resume in all caps or with lots of bold type—that's too much. I like to see pleasant design and lack of errors (misspelled words, dirty copy). I also like to see work experience before their education, and it's very helpful if they include personal information although it's rarely if ever done. It seems as if people are afraid to let you know who they are—single, married, kids, hobbies, volunteer work. I also like having a short introductory letter and a call from the person before he or she sends a resume. So many resumes come to me by email and fax these days that I don't remember if I've already talked to them or not. If I receive a resume without a letter or call, I don't take it seriously. I also have everyone fill out an application, too, for several reasons, but mainly to see the person's handwriting. I think it's a reflection of the individual's self-esteem and respect. The messier the handwriting, the more likely her desk will look the same, which usually (but not always) indicates the person's ability to prioritize and stay organized."

910. Allen Shirley, director and trou-bleshooter, construction company: "In a resume, the thing I look for most is an indication that the person is willing to take ownership of his job and make decisions. This is usually indicated by the jobs he has had and maintained. So much of the work I do requires that you not only have the knowledge but be willing to make decisions and live with them. I deal with conflict every day and try to be a part of the solution to end the problem; I expect that of people I hire. Lots of people want the job but don't want to have to make decisions. Some resumes show the person as a 'gunslinger'—that is a bad thing. Impulsiveness isn't good. I want to see a record of processing the available data, making a decision, and moving on to the next issue—and not getting personally involved with the problems. It's only business, and no one is going to get shot in the morning over decisions made today."

911. Lisa Hamilton, editorial coordinator, FabJob.com Ltd.: "Here are some 'things not to do' that I observed during our last round of hiring:

- Submitting a resume as an email attachment when the ad specifically says 'Include your resume in the body of an email. Please do not submit attachments.' If someone is not willing to follow instructions at this stage, what would that person be like as an employee?

- Addressing the cover letter to 'Dear Sirs.' The founders, president, CEO, and majority shareholders of our company are women. So are the two staff members who review all the resumes. 'Dear Sirs' may be acceptable when corresponding with a few stodgy law firms, but it isn't cool when contacting a publishing company in the twenty-first century.

- Referring to our company as 'fabjobs.com.' That's not our company name. Yet it's surprising the number of people who want to work as copy editors who make this basic mistake. (This is more than just a typo to us since that domain name was bought by a cybersquatter trying to capitalize on our site's popularity. We don't expect a job applicant to know why something bugs us; we just expect someone who's going to be responsible for ensuring our information is published correctly not to misspell our company name!)

- Misspelling 'details' (as detials) or addressing the letter to 'Linda' instead of 'Lisa.' But our favorite was: 'As I would very much like to develop a relationship with Fabio, I am willing to be flexible...' Thanks for the interesting visual, but we don't know Fabio!

• What impresses me is someone who takes the time to write us a brief personal letter explaining what she likes about FabJob.com and specifying how her experience is a fit with what we are looking for. So many people send generic letters, it is a real treat to find someone who has taken the time to learn something about us."

912.

Robin Leach, *Lifestyles of the Rich and Famous*: "Turn-on: legitimate experience in the field being hired for. Turn-off: personal interests and exaggerations. You look for initiative and enthusiasm, diligence and dedication."

913.

Elizabeth Frost Knappman, co-owner, New England Publishing Associates: "I look for someone with the skills I want someone to have. Let's say I'm looking for an editorial assistant—I like someone who fits with what my company does, has publishing experience, maybe computer skills, education (a master's in a related subject would impress me), and someone who loves to read. I look for experience, background, and skills. I don't like it when someone, in desperation, tries to oversell himself. An example would be a college dropout or someone right out of high school who says he's perfect for my editorial assistant job. A lot of our time is spent troubleshooting, and this person won't have the people skills or tact to deal with people without offending them. When someone tries to oversell, it means that he doesn't understand what we do."

914. Wendy Corson, EMT: "I dislike resumes that are multiple pages. I think they should always be on good-quality white paper and should be plain and concise. I immediately trash the ones with misspellings or cutesy fonts. Also, I don't really like 'Objective' statements because they state the obvious."

915. Tom Swan, energy manager, Pasadena Independent School District: "I am always impressed by the general appearance of the resume...when it's presented, does it catch my eye? One that's striking and appealing to the eye automatically moves up a little in my estimation. I also like a fairly short summary on a resume. I can call references, etc. to check further, but I don't want to read several pages to find out something about the individual. And, resumes that are accompanied by a portfolio are impressive."

916.

Gina Bradley, sales director: "I like an enthusiastic cover letter that tells me something about the person's accomplishments and achievements. I also am impressed by job consistency. A turn-off would be a resume that shows the person had too many jobs in a short period of time."

917.

David Garrett, program manager/chemical engineer, New Orleans: "I look at their experience and how they described it, which tells me if they know what they're talking about. Do they have the skills I need? Qualitatively, do I believe they have sufficient skills levels in that technology? How well do they communicate that in a written format? Then I look at the person's work history and see if the work history supports the skill he claims to have. I look to see if he has worked at any company where I know someone and can check them out. Basically, I'm looking at a resume with three things in mind: Does it make sense? Do I believe it? Are his skills what I need? What turns me off is the inverse. If I can't understand the resume or it's confusing, boom, I'm done. If it's vague or too short, I'm also done with it. I once got a resume that was thirty pages long, and everyone in the office looked at it and laughed at it, but that was as far as that resume got. No way we would interview that person."

918.

Tessie Patterson, co-owner of Patterson & Murphy Public Relations: "I really like basic—experience that's listed briefly and simply, last job first. I don't like bombastic language—keep it simple and skip the employment jargon that really says nothing. (Recently, I saw a resume that was the worst thing I'd ever seen. Too wordy, no organization, no focus!)"

919.

Trey Speegle, art director of *Us Weekly* magazine, New York: "Resumes are boring animals by nature, and no one cares much about them, but they serve a useful purpose. I hate when they are badly designed (natch) and also if they are over-designed (tiny, tiny type, etc.) or not designed at all. There's a fine line between looking like you've put some effort into it and appearing *obsessed* by presenting yourself in a 'distinctive' way. The tone has to be right. Some people go overboard in making themselves appear unique—colored paper, stickers, cute typeface, etc. Misspellings are a huge red flag in the publishing industry (maybe you can't spell, but don't you know a copy editor?). A resume has to be to the point, yet impressive. Padding or over-explaining responsibilities, if you've only worked at Kinko's or have been a summer intern, is a no-no. Trying too hard is the worst mistake you can make. A resume should reflect who you are and what you've done, but it doesn't have to say *everything*! As an architect once said, 'The nail doesn't have to be the whole house.'"

920. Robert Schiff, president, photowow.com, Los Angeles, California: "I quickly trash any resumes that contain misspellings, punctuation errors, and inconsistencies in the overall layout of the resume. An applicant has one or two pages to represent himself or herself. All the above should be perfect. If the applicant does not have the time to check for these errors, I don't have the time to read his/her resume. What I look for is experience and skills for the job. I also look at the amount of time spent at previous jobs. If an applicant never holds a job for more than two years, it's not worth our time to train that person."

921.

Paul Kelly, M.D.: "I think the organization of the resume—the actual layout—is as important as what the resume says. I need to be able to scan the resume and gather information. That way, I know very quickly if the qualifications are appropriate."

922.

Blair Pittman, author/photographer: "Resumes are so stuffy and formal. I would like to see in parentheses, maybe on a special job, something like (sure was fun). Just liven it up a bit."

923.

Clarence Chandler, petroleum engineer and company president: "Three criteria that influence whether I read the entire resume or dispatch it quickly to File 13 are: Keep it to one page. Keep it simple. Don't embellish your accomplishments."

924.

Marian Smithson, Boston socialite: "When I hire someone to work in the home environment, my advice is to really delve into the prior place of employment because you can't judge a book by its cover. Care and caution are key. You can't be too trustful. Remember, too, that companies are so limited as to what they can say as to why someone left their employment. Even when someone interviews well, her paperwork seems appropriate, and her personality is upbeat, you may come across a master forger (I did). Look at the resume long and hard, check to see if the information is legitimate, and you may be able to prevent the mistake of hiring a thief."

925. Jami Appenzeller, manager of the National Personal Training Institute in Virginia/Delaware and Pennsylvania: "My main thing with resumes is that I like when people seem easy to relate to. Not too outgoing or boastful (wanting to run the company soon!) but clearly confident, and not too 'perfect' for the job (like they just researched 'how to write a resume' for the very job I'm trying to fill), and natural, willing to learn but a person who has a lot to bring to the table, including just good honest work ethic. For some reason, natural and real resumes are much more appealing to me than the ones that look like a pro wrote it for them. I can't get a 'feel' for what the person is like from that kind of resume. I like to read intros to resumes that seem sincere and from the heart. Even if the individual isn't quite perfect for the job, it's nice to get a glimpse of what might come of this person."

926. Gabriela Baeza Ventura, executive editor of Arte Publico Press, Houston: "Since we are a bilingual press, one thing that always stands out is a person's knowledge of Spanish, as well as the listing of some book that they may have worked on. What turns me off are the lists and lists of people whom a person has worked with. I prefer to see this through books (final projects)."

927. Dennis Doughty, manager of Evin Thayer Photography Studio: "What turns me on in a resume is having words spelled correctly, having a resume that's together—with dates, contact names, and no space left blank. What turns me off is handwriting that cannot be read, not having information on previous employment, dates, etc."

928.

Spiker Davis, D.D.S., Cosmetic Dental Associates: "The main thing that turns me on is someone who says they like working with people. Since my business is so people-oriented, this is a must, and I like it when I see it on the resume versus I have to drag it out of them. I also like to see that they have self-confidence, and someone shows that on the resume. The number one turn-off for me is to see that they have worked at lots of different places and that they keep switching jobs."

929. Brett Belmarez, school superintendent: "My turn-on (in a resume) is when a person can tell you all about himself and his qualifications in a clear and succinct manner. The turn-off is when an applicant submits a portfolio when one wasn't asked for. Portfolios are braggadocio. The applicant is assuming that the employer has the time to weed through all of the contents to find an employee."

930. Donna Pate, senior editor, Service Corporation: "Big turn-off: a resume that contains handwritten corrections, crossed-out text, etc. as if the person were too lazy to generate a revised/updated resume. Another turn-off: A resume containing obvious spelling and grammatical errors, which indicates a lack of care/attention to detail. Good stuff: succinct summations of accomplishments and ways the individual benefited former employers. I want to know: What can you do for me? How can you help my business?"

931. Jack Townsend, attorney: "Two rules for resumes: (1) short and (2) short. Two pages max. This is for professional services resumes when you're looking for a job in a profession (lawyers, accountants, etc.). The resume must contain something that makes it stand out; otherwise, it will be discarded. By contrast, if it is an application for an academic position, or the resume is used for background to introduce a speaker, it might be longer."

932.

Michael Lewis, editor, Career Press: "I'm busy and don't have the patience to sift through nonsense. A resume has to be clean, easy-to-read, with info needed readily available."

933.

Evin Thayer, professional photographer, Houston, Texas: "For me, some resume turn-ons are enthusiasm and willingness to learn and job continuity. When a person has held the same job for at least three or four years (longer is even better), it tells me that they are loyal to the company and don't job-hop. I like to know the reason they want to work for me—that's helpful, along with what they specifically envision doing here. Also, how can that person make this business better by his presence? I prefer not to have to train them in the business, so any skills they can bring to the table that I don't have to teach gets my attention."

934.

Mary Morgan, department store hiring manager: "What I like is a resume that has been designed with the job in mind, and that represents the job candidate well, for the job she is seeking. It should be fashioned appropriately, and the material within it arranged so that the hiring manager gets a look immediately at the parts that will interest her most. A smart resume writer will make her resume the best it can be for the job candidate's current situation. What I don't like is a resume that uses 'keywords' inappropriately, which tells me the person is trying to give the impression she's familiar with my industry even though she's a total novice. Also, I dislike messy resumes—I'll throw those away in a heartbeat."

935.

Scott McMann, director of food-services employees, restaurant: "I like resumes that have pertinent parts easily displayed—I don't like to have to hunt all over the resume to see if the person has had a restaurant job. I also have a built-in prejudice against resumes that look bad, as if the toner on the printer needed to be changed, or the resume was crumpled up before it came to me."

936. John Shin, area manager, proposal development/SBC Proposal Center, Anaheim, California: "Resume turn-ons: Easy to read—succinct, well-written, clear layout, short but substantial with meaningful descriptions, one to two pages. Coherent body of experience showing a consistent set of skills and meaningful career arc—a handful of good stints at jobs lasting a few years at least. Skills and experience that support and validate each other. Good education record—a degree in a respectable liberal arts/humanities field from a solid institution to me implies training in critical thinking, research, and writing, and often means more to me than a vocational degree that may be directly relevant to the job. Resume turn-offs: Hard to read—small print, cramped, confusing layout, long descriptions full of jargon and acronyms, more than two pages. Too short and not enough info. Long, rambling list of random job experiences implying restlessness and instability. Long descriptions of skills with no supporting evidence or no correlation with descriptions of experience (e.g., 'I have strong web design skills' but web design is not mentioned in the work experience or training/education). Cute gimmicks. Spelling/grammatical errors and neologisms (e.g., 'impact,' 'interface,' 'task,' used as verbs, etc.)"

937. Jean Hardy, owner/general manager, Front Street Books, Terlingua, Texas: "In a resume, I look for clarity and precision and an opening statement that relates to the position for which the person is applying. What doesn't work at all for me is an obviously padded, overblown resume. And a pet peeve: mistakes in spelling and grammar."

938. Rebecca Covey, hair salon owner: "Don't use your cover letter to enthuse about the employer's company. We get tired of that. A resume should show what you can do for me, how many clients you'll bring with you from your last job."

939.

Darryl Huel, jewelry store owner: "In your cover letter, put a P.S. after your closing to draw attention to one last thing. This always catches my eye and may make me call you in for an interview. In your P.S., be sure to say something about how your skills are great for the job being advertised."

940.

Kathleen Hobe, publishing manager: "I hate to see resumes that sound pompous. Don't overdo patting yourself on the back. It is important to tell what you can do—your skills—but don't just give a string of adjectives. Give facts."

941. Sonia Hilton, real-estate company owner: "In a resume I look for signs that a person is tenacious, ambitious, and will work the numbers. For me, a bad sign is lack of attention to detail in getting the resume done right, with the required information."

942. Robert Dayton, financial planner: "I like it when someone sends in a resume right after an ad has been placed. That's impressive. After a few days, I have so many resumes in response to an ad that they get lost in the shuffle. What I don't like to see on a resume is a lack of basic information. You need to talk about what you did on jobs you've had."

943. Monty Smith, importer: "In resumes, I'm glad when someone bothers to give a full-fledged skill-set description. I hate resumes that give lots of personal information, which makes me wonder where that person has been for the past two decades. That stuff went out with covered wagons!"

944. Karen Brin, high school principal: "I like to see a polished resume that answers all the logical questions. I dislike resumes that try to 'trick' the reader into thinking the person has skills that fit an educational environment when that's obviously not the case."

945.

Doug Thompson, CPA: "When I'm hiring, I review resumes in a hurry. I want to find something that tells me the person is reliable, and I put a lot of stock in the cover letter. If it sounds interesting and the person comes across well, I'll call for an interview."

946. Mina McGown, human resources director: "I like to see a strong job history that tells me the person has done this kind of work and won't require lots of retraining. I don't like to see a resume that's all over the map, making it hard to tell what the person actually did."

947. Tony Cisneros, TV producer: "In resumes, I look for people who are ambitious, hardworking, and have excellent people skills. I don't like silly statements such as 'I watch a lot of TV so I want to work for a TV station' or 'I don't know anything about TV, but I know I'd be great as an editorial coordinator.' Don't test my patience."

948. Dinah Simone, health club owner: "I like to see enthusiasm in a resume and cover letter. What I hate to see is boasting that has nothing to back it up. Does the job candidate think she can trick me?"

949. Justin Li, graphic artist: "When I'm hiring for my group, I don't like resumes that puff up the education or skills. If the person took a weekend course on 'how to do a webpage,' I'm not fooled into thinking she's a 'webpage expert.'"

950. Liam Smithers, architect: "Don't send me a resume that looks like a mess. We're in the business of making things look great! I like to see an immaculately presented resume, with clarity of material and design."

951. Sara Garrity, office manager: "I want evidence that the person matches the job description very closely. My favorite resume is one that seems to bubble with the enthusiasm of the person who prepared it—it makes me eager to meet the job candidate, and I'm certainly going to invite that individual in for an interview. I am disappointed, however, when the person doesn't live up to the resume. Immediately, I assume the resume was prepared by someone other than the job candidate if the person I'm interviewing just bungles and mumbles and fidgets and has little to say for herself."

27.

Make the Most of Your Headhunter Experience

Using a recruiter can make a great deal of difference in ratcheting up the level, speed, size, and efficiency of your job search. There are several ways you can maximize the experience. Here are tips for making the most of your relationship with a headhunter and making your resume pay great dividends:

952. With a professional recruiter, you can take advantage of having the services of someone who focuses full time, year after year, on the job market. A recruiter familiarizes herself with your background and knows how to present you to a potential employer. Suggestions she makes are designed to help you land interviews and a job.

You can even let the headhunter use her experience to negotiate you a better salary (if you get an interview or a job offer, and the subject of salary comes into play). But don't become complacent because you have a recruiter working for you. You must continue to work for yourself; you are your own best advocate.

953. Listen to the advice of a recruiter when you decide how soon you should start interviewing if you're moving to a new location. A staff-level employee may need to begin about eight weeks in advance, whereas a person in management or higher should start at least three months in advance.

954. If your current employer offers you more money once you announce that you're leaving, meet with your recruiter to discuss this matter. Counteroffers are a stopgap measure to smooth a heavy workload, but accepting one will put you on the short list of temporary employees.

Your disloyalty (threatening to quit) may be rewarded by termination the first time there are reductions in the workforce or restructuring. Your boss won't forget. A recruiter will probably make this point: Do you want to work at a place that forces you to threaten to quit in order to get a raise? Why did they do this? Apparently, the company needed a few months of labor from you because it couldn't do without your skills in the short-term; usually, though, your supervisor will look for and find a way to eliminate you eventually.

955.

Understand how a recruiter's business works. Recruiters (often called headhunters) identify and recruit qualified candidates who have skills and expertise that client companies need to achieve their business goals. In most cases, the client company pays the recruiter, but recruiters must develop relationships with both job candidates and client companies in order to produce results. You can work with more than one recruiter if you want to.

956. Introduce yourself to a recruiter and make her aware of your background and your career interests. Ask her to keep you in mind for job opportunities. Express your degree of flexibility: Would you take a job in a related field? Do you want only one kind of position? Are you chiefly interested in going to work, or do you have other job requirements?

Get to know a headhunter before you actually start looking for a job. That way, you'll already have a professional relationship established when you do need to job-search, or when the recruiter sees an outstanding opportunity, she may call you to see if it interests you.

957. Do everything you can to assist your recruiter(s). Provide information as needed, and return calls and emails promptly when she contacts you. Show the headhunter how professional you are so that she is able to represent you efficiently—and so that she has firsthand experience that she can relate ("each time I email Amanda, she answers me the same day").

958.

If you have a job right now but are conducting a job search, limit your dealings with search firms to two or three that specialize in your area of expertise. This gives you enough advocates working on your behalf without significant overlap.

959.

Ask a recruiter to check into a company that you know you want to work for, even it you don't think it has any openings. She can check around to see what she can find out. Be ready to tell the recruiter the position you're interested in, and identify the hiring manager, if you can. The recruiter will probably send your resume to that person's attention and act on your behalf as an intermediary. You can follow up to introduce yourself after the resume has arrived; express your desire to work for the company and emphasize the value and talents you can bring to it.

960.

If you're looking for a job in several different parts of the country, work with experts in the respective areas.

961.

While you're working with a headhunter, continue to contact your network of personal and professional contacts for job leads. Don't just sit back and wait for the headhunter to do your work and solve your problems.

962.
If you're offered a job for less money than you make right now, talk to the headhunter about the pros and cons. The job may have a lower base but excellent potential for bonuses and commissions. Or you may be trading stress for more balance in your life. Your headhunter will probably explain the biggest disadvantage of going this route: When you take a step back in salary and responsibilities, you will have to work hard to regain your prior situation.

963.
Don't name a number for salary when you interview with a client company of the employment agency you're working with. If the company representative asks you about your salary expectations, tell them that you want the job, you're qualified for it, and that you want them to make you a fair offer based on your ability to contribute to the company.

964. Don't work with an agency that won't return your calls after you have sent in your resume.

965. Even if you work in a non-traditional industry that rarely requests resumes, you need a record of your employment history to submit to recruiters and employers. You can call it a resume or a fact sheet, but do include companies you've worked for, cities where you've worked, positions held, dates of employment, and duties and responsibilities you performed. You need to be able to make this information available in order to complete employment applications or produce a resume if someone requests one.

966. Listen to your recruiter and follow instructions. If she tells you the potential employer wants you to fax a resume, do so. If email or mail is preferred, then follow that route.

Apply the suggestions that your recruiter thinks will help you get a job. If, for example, the headhunter wants you to beef up your knowledge on the company prior to going on an interview, make your first stop the Internet. Look for information about the firm and then check out the industry and the company's competitors. A second resource is the public library; go in person or use its dial access system. The library will have trade journals with information on the industry—and you can also look for articles that mention the particular company.

967. Ask the recruiter to prepare you for that big job interview. He can brief you on questions you may be asked, give you tips on interview taboos, and tell you what to do during and after the interview to help seal the deal. For example, he may suggest that you ask the interviewer if he has any questions or concerns about your ability to do the job, and that gives you the opportunity to address these. Also, you should remember to ask for the job. Follow up by writing a thank-you note to the interviewer just as soon as you return home. Don't call and bug the interviewer: "When are you making your decision? I thought you said you'd call me last week. Didn't you think I did a good job on the interview? Do you think I'm the best of the people you interviewed? Do you think I'll get the job? How much money will I make? You forgot to tell me about benefits and vacation—and sick days." Pestering a hiring manager or being presumptuous leaves an awful impression that suggests you would be a problem employee.

968.

Give your recruiter the leads you picked up at a job fair. Indicate which companies sound good to you. At a job fair, you can gather information about different companies, find leads, and ask your recruiter to follow up. Talk to as many different companies as possible when you attend a job fair because time is limited.

969.

Don't drive your recruiter crazy. Some clients call twenty times a day to ask questions: "Have you found me anything yet? How long is this going to take? Do you think you will find me a job? Can I call you back in an hour to see if you've found me anything?"

Even if you're just communicating by email, several emails in one day is overkill. Your recruiter won't forget about you. It's OK to check in with him or her about once a week, but don't be more aggressive than that. The headhunter has your number and will contact you the minute he has something for you.

970. Ask your recruiter to help you spiff up your resume if you're trying to get a job in a new field where you have related but not identical experience. Let's say you're interested in working in the human resources department of a large city hospital; you have a psychology degree and several years of administrative and clerical experience. Since human resources is made up of recruiting, employee relations, training, and compensation and benefits, you can see that it's not hard to parlay your forms of experience into the field.

971. Get your recruiter to give you tips on any aspect of the job hunt that you feel shaky about. For example, one job-hunting candidate was anxious about an upcoming phone interview until she turned to her recruiter, who offered these tips: First, establish your skills, interest, and qualifications. Second, try to get an office visit. A phone interview is as serious as any first interview, so it's important to research the company so that you know what it does, how big it is, and who its major competitors are. Tell the hiring manager how you can help him and how your skills can benefit his company. Express interest in the job, and ask for an in-person visit. (Try standing up during the phone interview; your voice will sound more confident and alert.)

972.

Ask your headhunter for information on the cost of living in the city where you're relocating. This will help when you're looking at a $60,000 job offer from a company in New York and you want to know if it's enough (you've lived well in Houston on $50,000 a year). The recruiter will tell you to calculate the cost of living anywhere by looking at the PPI—Producer's Price Index, a detailed analysis of cost of housing, food, clothing, taxes, etc. Each city has an index based on 100, the average. For example, Houston's is 98, and New York City's is 138. Based on these statistics, you would need a salary of about $75,000, not $60,000, for the NYC job to be comparable.

973.

You can ask a recruiter how to respond (during an interview) when you're asked a question that you perceive as biased, such as: Do you plan to have children? Probably, the recruiter will tell you that question is illegal. Title VII of the Civil Rights Act of 1964 prohibits an employer from considering race, color, religion, sex, or national origin in employment or discharge. But you still may be asked an inappropriate question. If someone asks if you plan to have kids, go to the root of the query: "I come to work regularly, I work hard, and I work the hours required."

974.
Ask your recruiter if you're not sure what the language in a job listing means. For example, let's say you see a position with a company that sounds like something you would like, but the listing asks for "a financial professional with computer skills," and you don't know what this means. Your recruiter will explain that "computer skills" refer primarily to software packages used, and in the case of financial professionals, this would refer to a basic level of competence in a spreadsheet package, word processing package, general ledger package, and a database management package. Once she translates the ad for you, you can decide if you have the right skills to apply for the job. Don't be afraid to call your headhunter and pick her brain on subjects like this.

Similarly, you may want to ask a recruiter to define the difference between the following types of skills often referred to in ads:

- What are functional skills? These are job functions such as performing audits, accounts payable, receivable, financial reporting, cost accounting.
- What are industry skills? These skills related to a specific industry in which you gained the functional skills: real estate, oil and gas, manufacturing, banking, etc.
- What are managerial skills? These skills relate to the level of management, number of employees reporting to you directly and indirectly, and remote locations under your responsibility.

- What are computer skills? These are software packages you can use. For example, an editor needs to know word processing.

28.

Do Your Resume Proud When You Interview

Be ready. Once you've mailed that resume, an interview could pop up any time, so it's a good idea to prepare yourself for that opportunity. Here are some tips for doing your resume proud in an interview:

975.
Research a company prior to the interview. Look on the Internet, and also check out information on the industry and the company's competitors. Go to the public library if you need to. Look for articles in newspaper and trade journals on the company and its industry. You can find the company's annual report, or find excerpts of it in Moody's and Standard and Poor's. On the Internet, you can find sections devoted to 10Ks, 10Qs, and other information on publicly held companies—use keywords EDGAR or Disclosure. Look at the library's industry guides for information on the company that you're researching.

Before the day of your interview, ask around to find out what others in the industry think of this company. This will give you a feel for the stability of the company and its position in the marketplace.

976.
Take a phone interview seriously. Increasingly, it's becoming common practice for employers to use phone interviews as a first-round screening device. The interviewer wants to check into your basic skills, your interest in the job and your qualifications. For you, it's an opportunity to pave your way to phase two—an office interview. This means you should treat the interview with the same seriousness you would give to an in-person interview.

Before a phone interview ends, express your interest in the job (if indeed you are interested). Ask for an office interview. Be professional and assertive. Smile so that you will sound friendly.

Whether an interview is in-person or on the phone, do make a point of telling the employer how you think you can help them. Pinpoint how your skills can benefit the company's overall efforts and the business itself. Don't be shy, and don't be abrasive. Do be forthright and confident.

977.
Dress well for an in-person interview. If you're in doubt about what to wear, dress up rather than dressing down. If you're male, wear a coat and tie for an interview. If you're female, a suit is perfect. The right clothing for an interview reflects your respect for the interviewer and his company. Then, when you're hired, you can wear the kind of office/work attire that is viewed as acceptable for that company. For example, a surgeon who usually wears "scrubs" in the operating room should not view this as garb that's appropriate for an interview. Also, don't wear gaudy colors, quirky outfits or cocktail attire. You want to look conservative, polished, and smooth. You can express your personal style *after* you get the job.

Before you go on an interview, have a friend or relative do a frank assessment, to ensure that you'll make a great first impression. Find out:
- Is your slip showing?
- Do your shoes look scuffed?
- Is the red power tie too thin?
- Has your mascara given you raccoon eyes?

- Are your clothes too tight, too old-fashioned, too dirty, too dandruff-strewn?
- Is your sport coat acceptable or should you wear a suit? (A suit!)
- How's your breath?
- Do your teeth look clean?
- Is your makeup better suited for a nightclub than the day lighting of an office?
- Do you look neat or disheveled?
- Are you underdressed?

Arrange for this checkup well in advance of interview time so that you can make upgrades if necessary. Don't let something totally superficial (wrong clothing, makeup, tie, teeth) keep you from getting a job you're qualified to have. Get your look spiffed up, along with your resume and interview skills, and if you're the right skill package for the job, you're probably going to land it.

978.
Be ready to answer logical questions. Think back on previous interviews and prepare yourself for the inevitable "What are your biggest strengths and weaknesses?" queries. You don't want to come across as "thrown" by the interviewer's questions, so go in there like a veteran of interviews, even if this is your first one ever. If you have very little experience being interviewed for jobs, talk to friends and family members and find out about common interview questions. Do all that you can to get yourself ready.

Don't name a figure when an interviewer asks you what salary you have in mind. Say that you're interested, that you believe you can do an excellent job, and that you would love to entertain a reasonable offer. Stating a figure can put you out of the running. If it's too high, the hiring manager may think you would be disappointed or turn down the job. If the figure you state is too low, you'll end up with a salary lower than he had planned to pay.

Respond to the "What is your biggest weakness?" question carefully. If you confess your weaknesses, you lose big (even though the interviewer and you both know that everyone has flaws). Just finesse your answer, or volunteer a benign weakness. You can say, "I used to be a perfectionist, but over the years, I have learned how to devote enough time to a project so that I can walk away from it and feel that I have done it well." In other words, if you admit a weakness, soften it up.

Don't answer the question "What would be your ideal job?" by saying that it's the one you're interviewing for. Instead, list standout parts of the job you are interviewing for, and point out ways that you think your skills make you the ideal person for the position. This question is just one more chance for you to underscore your suitability for the position, and how you are by far the best candidate.

Use the "What is your biggest strength?" question as a springboard for selling yourself. Zoom into a description of your excellent qualities and job skills so that the interviewer walks away extremely glad that he asked that question.

Don't feel compelled to answer illegal questions, such as "Do you plan to have children?" Under Title VII of the Civil Rights Act, this question discriminates against women and married people, both of which the Act protects. Instead, you can respond to what's at the base of the kid question: Will you dependably work the hours required? Reassure the interviewer that you are ready and willing to work the days and times required for the particular job. Probably not a good idea, however, to say, "I refuse to answer that" when the subject comes up, if it does.

Tell the employer what your religion is *only* if your religious beliefs will affect your work: for example, if being a Buddhist means you can't work certain hours, or you have to take off certain days during the year. Always discuss special situations in advance; don't just spring something on him as you're walking out the door one day to attend a religious service. A good employee bears in mind that the business wheels keep on turning even when she is out of the office, so follow good form and keep supervisors advised of what you must do out of the office and when you will need to miss work.

979. Focus on the job you want and the company that is offering the job. Don't put any emphasis on your personal life. The interviewer wants to hear you explain how your skills and experiences make you highly qualified for this job, and he also expects to hear that you want to make a contribution to the company.

980. Bring up personal information only if it explains why you can perform the job better or how you have special insight. For example, if you apply to work at an international company, it would be appropriate to mention that you have traveled widely. Or if you want to work for a company involved in oil exploration/production, the fact that you grew up in the oil patch is definitely worth bringing up. It makes you an insider.

Explain a health situation only if it affects your successful fulfillment of the job duties. In the best-case scenario, you would always attend your job faithfully and perform your duties well. But if you know you will need to take off work for a health matter (or something else), discuss this during an interview.

981.

Feel free to improvise if you're asked a technical question you don't know the answer to. The interviewer may just want to gauge your logic and deductive reasoning, so if you don't know an exact answer, just reason it out and come up with a response that sounds logical based on the knowledge you do have. In other words, it's OK to guess.

982. Focus on selling your personality. Focus on the experience that you bring to the table. Focus on your skills that you know are noteworthy. Remember, the biggest-strength question is an invitation to brag about yourself. So do exactly that. But don't sound arrogant, saying things like, "I'm better than anyone else in the computer field at writing code." Even if it's true, saying so sounds cockier than you want to come across during an interview.

But don't try to be lovably flaky when you're being interviewed. A hiring manager rates stability very high on his list of desirable qualities, and a clown usually doesn't strike anyone as dependable.

983. Make sure you don't interview the interviewer—big mistake! Instead, sell yourself and your experience, and remember to show that you want the job.

During the interview, ask the interviewer about the company's background and its goals. Focus on telling the interviewer what you can do for him. You don't want to turn it into a question-answer session, with you being the one firing questions. If you interview the interviewer, what have you accomplished? He will leave the table not knowing you much better than he did before, and when he stacks up the candidates to compare them, the lack of a good impression probably won't make you the winner.

Show the interviewer your desire to work with him and the rest of the workforce to serve the company's customers. Try to work some mention of how well you get along with people and how service-minded you are into the conversation. If you have a good customer rapport story you can relate, this is the perfect time.

Express interest in adding value to the company by being an excellent, skilled employee. Set your sights on proving to the interviewer that you are the answer to her business's problems. However, if you know that the company is experiencing problems, don't go into that sensitive area.

Talk about "career progression" if the interviewer asks why you're changing careers. Don't go into a sob story of "burnout"—no one wants to hear it. If you are asked, 'Why don't you stay in the field in which you have been successful?' simply talk about how you've read that most people change careers seven to eight times in a lifetime, and you view the change as a progression in your career, not an abrupt detour. A step up, in other words.

984. Do not ask about salary or benefits on an interview. This is a huge, gigantic, gauche, horrible–awful mistake that can alienate a hiring manager. Presuming that you will get a job offer just makes you look silly and naïve. A lack of sophistication is a bad thing. Remember, first you have to convince the hiring manager that the company should make you an offer.

Do discuss benefits and salary if and when you're offered a job. That is perfectly acceptable after the hiring manager opens up that line of talk by making you an offer.

985.

Don't demonize others when you're being interviewed. You should show that you're a team player, not a self–serving viper. If you treat business like a war game, there's a good chance you will dive-bomb off the candidate list. No one likes a troublemaker; most companies already have one on staff that they wish they could get rid of.

986.

Toward the end of the interview, ask the interviewer if he has any concerns about your ability to do the job. If concerns are expressed, address these honestly and carefully. Reassure the interviewer that you have the "right stuff" for this position. Be upbeat, smiley, and enthusiastic. Don't express doubts (even if you have some). If you get the job, you can then ask for help in firming up your skills.

A few days before the interviewer is supposed to call to give you The Big Answer, call and ask if there are questions that may have come up, and express your interest in answering them. At this time, reassert your interest and say that you believe you are especially well qualified for the job. Don't worry what he may think of your "assertiveness." If you get the job, you'll know that he liked your proactive approach, and if you don't get it, what does it matter what the interviewer thought of your being aggressive?

Ask the interviewer when he thinks a decision will be made and when you can expect to hear from someone. Don't be demanding. That kind of "attitude" sends a very bad signal, and your resume may be tossed into the trash before you even get out the door.

987. Focus on the job (not money) and get hired. If you have dollar signs in your eyes during the entire interview and pepper every sentence with mentions of money, you'll sound either desperate or mercenary. Either way, you will pale in comparison to candidates who put less emphasis on the bottom-line figure. If you get a job offer and you don't like the money, you can ask for more. You may or may not get it, but you certainly won't get it if you don't ask. Many companies have a salary range for a certain job, and compensation for that position must fall within that range. It's OK to try to negotiate, but don't get obnoxious or the job offer may be withdrawn.

988. Maintain a keen awareness of the Big Four: people are hired for attitude, ability, aptitude, and experience. Show your willingness and eagerness to do the job, and make it clear that you would fit in with the team and the company. Your experience represents industry skills and functional skills that you have gained in previous positions you have held. Aptitude is your perceived ability to learn and transfer knowledge from one area to another. The interviewer's perception is all that matters. If he believes that you cannot do these things, even if he is wrong, you won't be made an offer. Most important of all is attitude—your enthusiasm for the job and the company will go a long way toward impressing an interviewer. Bottom line: To land a job, you must convince the interviewer that you want the position, that you can do a terrific job, and that you will grow and learn and contribute to the company.

989. Don't tell a hiring manager what's what. One supervisor says, "I hate it when I hand someone an application to fill out and she takes out a resume, hands it to me, and tells me that all the information I need is on her resume so she won't need to complete an application. Wait a minute—isn't that my call?"

990. Don't try to run things. One hiring manager says, "It's awful when someone shows up thirty minutes early and expects the interview to begin right then. Or when someone shows up late for the scheduled interview—that's the kiss of death. The absolute worst is not having a resume at all."

29.

The Resume Worked—Quit with Style!

Believe it or not, there's an art to quitting a job. You can do it with flair, or you can do it with fizzle. Think of yourself as being in a celebratory mode—you sent out a great resume, you nabbed someone's attention, and you got the job you wanted! But now you're facing one of life's most unsettling moments—having to go into your boss's office and announce that you're leaving.

For most people, this is an emotional time. You're nervous. You hate leaving a job you were good at and good friends you worked with. You have mixed feeling about making the move to another job. At the same time, change is good—or at least that's what you keep telling yourself. Scary, all right, but it's a scary world.

What's the best way to quit? Here are some tips for making your way out the door with as much grace and style as possible—and the assurance, perhaps, that your current supervisor will give you a good reference.

991. Hand deliver a short letter of resignation documenting the date you have given notice and what will be your last day of employment. Thank the employer for the opportunity to work there and wish him continued success.

992. Don't go into elaborate detail in your letter of resignation. Don't feel compelled to give a reason for leaving in your letter of resignation. Do give at least two weeks' notice.

993. Be professional when you hand in the letter of resignation. Be polite. Never burn bridges. Just because you're quitting doesn't give you license to tell your supervisor how much you dislike him or hate the company. Walk out the door with your reputation intact; that's the most important asset you have.

994. If asked why you're quitting, use a phrase such as "leaving to pursue other opportunities." Don't let your supervisor put you on the spot. He may try to get you to reveal things that bothered you about the job. Why should you do that? Don't indulge in full disclosure about coworkers or supervisor now that you are leaving. Remember that any negative comments you make when you're quitting can come back to haunt you later.

995. Bear in mind that the person you hand your letter of resignation is probably the one who will later be contacted for a reference on you. Don't leave him with a bad feeling about the way that you quit. Be generous, fair, and respectful. If you ask your supervisor for a letter of recommendation, don't do it the day you turn in your resignation. Wait a few days. Don't ask for a letter of recommendation when you quit if you know that there's not even a slim chance that your supervisor liked you or would say anything positive about you.

996. Don't drag your feet in performing your work after you resign. Continue just like you would if you were staying. Make sure you don't leave loose ends that will be caught after you leave—and remarked upon. The "leaving-job" syndrome can make some employees lazy and careless, and naturally this irritates supervisors and coworkers.

997. If you're resigning because your resignation was requested after another employee made a statement about you, ask what sort of reference your employer plans to give you. He may say that he will release only your title and dates of employment. Ask if he is going to say that you were fired because you need to know this in case it comes up during a future job interview. If you can find other references at the same company, use those to help mitigate any possible damage this employer may do.

998. Don't make snide comments to another employee who just happens to be leaving the company before your departure date. One boss tells of an employee who wrote on a coworker's goodbye card signed by the whole staff: "No fair! You're getting out of this awful place before me!" You can be sure that employee won't get a good recommendation from her boss who read what she wrote.

999. If your supervisor refuses to write a letter of recommendation or serve as a reference, ask if he will give employment verification. Typically, this must be done on company letterhead. The law says that a former employee does not have to do anything for you except verify your title and dates of employment; this was originally intended to protect the privacy of employees. The part that's missing is the job description. Your former employer doesn't have to release this kind of information, but you may be able to solve the problem by writing a description of what you did when you worked there and sending this to the human resources manager for editing. That may remove the obstacle.

1000. If you're quitting because the job wasn't what the hiring manager said it would be, it's not going to change anything to address this matter when you resign. After you were hired and the job changed, you could have asked, but now, your choice is leave or stay. When you look for a job, you can tell prospective employers that the job was not as represented during your initial interview. The interviewer may or may not believe you.

BIBLIOGRAPHY

Careers4U.com. Computer Placement online. 20 May 2003 www.careers4u.com/resume.htm

"Career Owl Resources." Career Owl Jobseeker Resources online. 11 July 2003 www.careerowl resources.ca/resumes

DeCarlo, Laura. "Is Your Resume Ready for All This Technology?" Competitive Edge Career Service online. 11 May 2003 www.acompetitiveedge. com/a_is_your.html

Jobweb.com. www.jobweb.com

"My Resume Writer." Chapman Services Group online. 1 July 2003 www.my-resume-writer.com

"Online resumes." Barnard Career Development online. 20 July 2003 www.barnard.columbia. edu/ocd/factsheets/onlineres.htm

"Polished Resumes." Career Marketing Techniques online. 1 June 2003 www. polishedresumes.com

Professional Association of Resume Writers and Career Coaches online. 15 August 2003 www.parw.com

Weddle, Peter D. *Internet Resumes: Take the Net to Your Next Job.* Manassas Park, VA: Impact Publications, 1998.

Yate, Martin John. *Cover Letters That Knock 'Em Dead, 5th Edition.* Avon, MA: Adams Media Corp, 2002.

ABOUT THE AUTHORS

Author, entrepreneur, and editor **Diane Stafford** has written six nonfiction books, *Potty Training For Dummies, Migraines For Dummies, The Encyclopedia of Sexually Transmitted Diseases, No More Panic Attacks: A 30-Day Plan for Conquering Anxiety, 40,001 Best Baby Names,* and *1000 Best Job Hunting Secrets.* All but the last two were coauthored with Stafford's daughter, Jennifer Shoquist, M.D.

Stafford also edits books and writes marketing materials for doctors. She has been editor-in-chief of five magazines, owner of two magazines, and has written hundreds of articles for various magazines. She has a B.A. summa cum laude from Sam Houston State University. Besides working as a freelance writer/editor, Stafford lives in Newport Coast, California.

Moritza Day is president and founder of Day West & Associates, Inc., a nationally known business and career–consulting firm. Putting her sales knowledge to work, she led her company to increase sales 500 percent over three years. Growing purely by market share, Day West & Associates, Inc. was named as number 23 of the Houston 100, the one hundred privately held firms having the greatest impact on Houston.

Moritza Day authored the workbook *Networking to Build Your Success*. She is also an in-demand speaker, sought out by professional organizations and universities. She has appeared on television and radio.

Day began her business career as an auditor with a Big 4 accounting firm and worked in internal audit for two major bank holding companies. Her sales career started at an international accounting/financial recruiting firm where she performed searches. Later she went on to head the South Texas region of the temporary division. Under her leadership, her branch was the firm's leading office in the country. She has a B.B.A in accounting and is a CPA. For fifteen years, Day has trained and motivated people, helping them realize their potential and maximize their skills, and translate that to substantially better career results. Her countless stories of success and learning opportunities mesh well with winning strategies of marketing and business development. Day's mission is to help individuals and organizations create and build success through business and professional development. She speaks on Networking for Your Success, Prospecting: Turning Cold Calls into Gold, and Negotiating So Everyone Wins–Especially You. Her website is www.daywestinc.com.